Computing in Musicology

A Directory of Research

Edited by

Walter B. Hewlett

Eleanor Selfridge-Field

Center for Computer Assisted Research in the Humanities

Menlo Park, CA

1990

© 1990 Center for Computer Assisted Research in the Humanities

Center for Computer Assisted Research in the Humanities
525 Middlefield Road, Suite 120
Menlo Park, CA 94025
XB.L36@Stanford.Bitnet

LIBRARY
ALMA COLLEGE
ALMA, MICHIGAN

Preface

Computing in Musicology is a digest of current activity related to musical scholarship. Its coverage spans activities in an ever-growing number of fields in music history, theory, composition, and performance, in computer and information sciences, in software engineering, and in numerous nooks and crannies of the hard sciences, mathematics, and psychology. Our main source of information is reports by our readers. It is their generous response and willingness to share their perspectives on work in progress that makes our publication possible. Information concerning prospective contributions is given at the back of this book.

This issue provides a close look at tools for the computational study of medieval and Renaissance repertories. This emphasis reflects both a significant number of important projects currently underway in this area and a significant, if brief, history of endeavor. Much attention to representation, printing, analysis, and even optical recognition have been devoted to this area.

Our report on standards covers some eminently important subjects, ranging from proposed extensions to the MIDI standard and the establishment of a compact disk plus MIDI (CD+M) standard to a glimpse of the first draft of a Standard Music Description Language and its text-encoding analogue, the TEI document format.

Our coverage of software for music printing extends this year to dance notation software and includes a large number of activities related to the development of software for theory, analysis, and composition. We also have a section on workstation projects.

We explore some of the non-technical issues related to data bases of text, note briefly a number of new bibliographical products on CD-ROM, report on releases of musical data and interactive compact disk (CD+I) products, and provide short reports on some dedicated applications.

This year's issue is heavily indebted to its many contributors, among whom we would especially like to thank the contributors of information on Special Topics and Technical Standards as well as the developers of software for music printing and dance notation, in the first case for their informative reports and in the second for their graphically meticulous output. Translations from the Greek were provided by Stephen Waite and Wilkins Poe. Susan Alexander, Barbara Barclay, Frances Bennion, Trudy Brassell, Clive Field, and Steven Rasmussen all provided valuable support in the production stage of the work. The material on music printing was collected and organized by Edmund Correia, Jr. We remain grateful to our many unnamed contributors and to those—such as Lelio Camilleri, Alan Marsden, Steven Page, Thomas Walker, and David Wessel—who keep us in touch with other parts of the world.

October 4, 1990   *Menlo Park, CA*

Table of Contents

News

Meetings

ACH/ALLC–1990 and 1991

"The New Medium" was the title of the joint meeting of the International Association for Literary and Linguistic Computing (its 17th) and the International Association for Computers and the Humanities (its 10th) held at the University of Siegen, Germany, from June 4-9, 1990. While no sessions on music were scheduled, there were several on manuscript studies, including "Early Manuscripts--Documentation and Information Exchange via Computer," chaired by Menso Folkerts of the Deutsches Museum in Munich, and "Medieval Manuscripts," chaired by Jacqueline Hamesse of the Université Catholique de Louvain.

Tempe, Arizona, will be the site of the 1991 joint meeting, "Making Connections." Arizona State University will serve as host institution for the event, scheduled for March 17-21. Enquiries may be addressed to Daniel Brink, Dept. of English, Arizona State University, Tempe, AZ 85287-0302.

AIM–1990

The fifth workshop on Artificial Intelligence and Music, scheduled for August 7 in Stockholm, was to include papers on cognitive musicology, expert systems, knowledge representation, neural computing, and AI-based tools for music research. Enquiries about the proceedings may be sent to Antonio Camurri (music@dist.dist.unige.it).

Increased participation by musicologists and ethnomusicologists is sought. For information about future workshops one may contact Mira Balaban, Gianni De Poli, Kemal Ebcioğlu, Goffredo Haus, Otto Laske, Marc Leman, or Christoph Lischka.

CMCCT–1990

A two-day meeting entitled "College Music Curriculum and Current Technology: Models for Application" took place at the University of Minnesota at Duluth on August 2-4, 1990. The keynote speakers were Fred T. Hofstetter (University of Delaware), chief architect of the Videodisk Music Series, and G. David Peters (CERL, University of Illinois), a co-author of the Schirmer book *Music Teaching and Learning*.

CMR–1991

A second conference on the use of computers in all branches of musical research is planned for the dates April 7-10 in Belfast, Northern Ireland. The meeting is modelled along the same lines as one held in Lancaster, England, in April 1988. Papers and software demonstrations are planned. For details, please contact Alan Marsden at the Department of Music, The Queen's University, Belfast BT7 1NN, Northern Ireland, UK.

ICMC–1990

Demonstration projects running on the Macintosh II, the Atari ST, and the Apollo and NeXT workstations were scheduled to take place at the International Computer Music Conference in Glasgow. The dates were September 10-15.

Among the papers scheduled were descriptions of the KANSEI Music System by Haruhiro Katayose and Seiji Inokuchi, of "Ensemble: An Object-Oriented Real-Time Performance System" by Lounette Dyer, "Pattern Matching as an Engine for the Computer Simulation of Musical Style" by David Cope, and "Conceptual Integrity in a Music Notation Interface" by Glendon Diener. A session was to be devoted to the use of computer music in developing the talents of the disabled.

Proceedings of the ICMC are available from the Computer Music Association, PO Box 1634, San Francisco, CA 94101-1634.

ICTM–1990

"Transcription of Traditional Music" was to be the theme of the study group on computer research, meeting under the auspices of the International Council for Traditional Music in Marseille, France, on September 29 and 30, 1990. Problems encountered in analysis and archiving of music in oral traditions are also frequently considered by the group. For information on the group's activities, please contact Helmut Schaffrath.

MIM–1990

"Musique et Assistance Informatique" was the title of the second international conference organized by the Laboratoire Musique et Informatique de Marseille and scheduled to take place between October 3 and 6. Papers and roundtables concerning compositional theory, modelling, musical representation, and other subjects were scheduled, and a software demonstration was planned. One of the scheduled talks was to be André Riotte's "Formalization and Mathematical/Computer Models of Musical Scores." Simultaneous translation into English or French was promised. Orders for the proceedings (in French) of the 1988 meeting, "Musical Structures and Information Technology," can be sent to Laboratoire MIM, 36 Bd Pardigon, F-13004 Marseille, France. The electronic address (Bernard Bel) is bel@frmop11.bitnet.

Music Publishing and Music Representation

An invited symposium on music publishing and music representation is currently being organized for the autumn of 1991 by John Chowning and Leland Smith at the Center for Computer Research in Music and Acoustics at Stanford University. Topics to be considered include on-demand publishing, interactive listening, audible scratch pads, optical scanning, and new domains of music research.

Periodicals

Array

Array, the quarterly newsletter of the Computer Music Association, has been expanded and upgraded with the Summer 1990 issue. Research notes, studio reports, and announcements of conferences, products, and publications are being sought for future issues. Submissions may be sent to Carla Scaletti (scaletti@novamail.cerl.uiuc.edu).

Computers in Music Research

Computers in Music Research is an annual publication first produced in the autumn of 1989 through the Wisconsin Center for Music Technology. Its editor is John William Schaffer. *CMR* carries articles, book reviews, research reports, and short news items. Many readers will find the seventeen-page bibliography appended to Bo Alphonce's retrospective article on "Computer Applications in Music Research" a helpfully concise resource. Individual subscriptions are $12, which may be sent to the Wisconsin Center for Music Technology, School of Music, University of Wisconsin, Madison, WI 53706.

EthnoForum

EthnoForum, a digest of information about work in ethnomusicology, is an online publication edited by Karl Signell at the Baltimore County campus of the University of Maryland. It carries timely and succinct notices about meetings, research projects, appointments, obituaries, and other items of professional and personal interest to ethnomusicologists. *EF* is well indexed and organized. Such finely crafted contributions as Mantle Hood's memorial and Jim Kippen's obituary for John Blacking, who died in January, rise far above the norm for electronic journalism. For details, send the message "GET WELCOME INFO" to LISTSERV@UMDD. Messages for inclusion may be sent to ETHMUS-L@UMDD with one of the following headers: DISCUSSION, NEWS, JOBS. Files for archiving may be sent to SIGNELL@UMDD.

Leonardo Music Journal

The editors of *Leonardo*, a journal devoted to the electronic arts, have announced the founding of a new *Leonardo Music Journal*. Annual publication will begin in 1991. Work combining the visual and sound arts will be of particular interest. For further information contact *Leonardo Music Journal*, Box 75, 1442A Walnut St., Berkeley, CA 94709.

MUSICUS

Musicus is the title of a semi-annual journal of computer-based music research published by the British Universities' Computers in Teaching Initiative designated Centre for Music (CTICM) at the University of Lancaster. Anthony Pople serves as editor. The journal concentrates on teaching applications and theories underlying them as well as curriculum issues. Lisa Whistlecroft's concise software directory (pp. 89-97) provides citations to reviews in the trade press.

The first issue carried three "user reports" on the music printing programs *HB Music Engraver*, *Professional Composer*, and *SCORE*. *Musicus* is distributed free of charge to all full-time academics in music departments in the UK. Others may subscribe for £10 a year. For further information please contact Lisa Whistlecroft (L.Whistlecroft@lancaster.ac.uk), the assistant editor, at CTICM, University of Lancaster, Lancaster LA1 4YW, UK.

General Articles

"Databases and the Practice of Musicology" by Walter B. Hewlett and Eleanor Selfridge-Field and "Computer-Based Approaches to Musical Data and Musical Analysis" by Mario Baroni and Eleanor Selfridge-Field will appear in the second volume of the *Atti del XIV Congresso della Società Internazionale di Musicologia (Bologna 1987)*, edited by L. Bianconi, A. Gallo, A. Pompilio, and D. Restani. Publication by Edizioni di Torino (via Alfieri 19, I-10121 Turin, Italy) is scheduled for the end of 1990.

John Rahn writes on "Processing Musical Abstraction: Remarks on LISP, the NeXT, and the Future of Musical Computing" in *Perspectives of New Music*, 28/1 (1989), 180-191.

John Roeder describes "A General-Purpose Object System for Music Graphics" in the *Proceedings of the 1989 International Computer Music Conference* (San Francisco, 1989), pp. 260-3.

John William Schaffer discusses "Intelligent Tutoring Systems: New Realms in CAI?" in *Music Theory Spectrum* 12/2 (1990).

"Reflections on Technology and Musicology" is an article by Eleanor Selfridge-Field that prefaces a report of the International Musicological Society's Study Group on Musical Data in *Acta Musicologica* 52/3 (1990), the journal of the IMS published by Bärenreiter Verlag.

Software Catalogues

Association for Technology in Music Instruction

More than 600 items are listed in the catalogue of computer programs for music education edited by Charles Boody and others and distributed by the Association for Technology in Music Instruction. The catalogue is available for $15 from ATMI, ISD 270, Evaluation Center 246, 1001 Highway 7, Hopkins, MI 55343.

Digital Arts and Technologies

Digital Arts and Technologies, Inc (21 Glen Ridge Road, Mahopac, NY 10541) publishes an annual *Musician's Music Software Catalog*. A two-year subscription is available for $5 ($10 for overseas orders). The company also offers telephone consultation (914-638-7949) and toll-free ordering (800-332-2251).

Micro-Music

An extensive catalogue of music software for IBM PC compatibles, Macintosh, Atari, Amiga, and other microcomputers is available free from Micro Music, Inc., Pinetree Plaza #17, 5269 Buford Highway, Atlanta, GA 30340.

Books and Dedicated Issues of Journals

Advances in Computing in the Humanities

Goffredo Haus is the guest editor of the next issue of *Advances in Computing in the Humanities*, a special number on music applications. There are three main parts to the book—a section of tutorials, a section on music processing, and a section of studio reports. Contributions include articles on music description by Otto Laske, Marc Leman, Antonio Camurri, and the editor, as well as a consideration of "Music Analysis by Computer: Concepts and Issues" by Eleanor Selfridge-Field and several pieces on signal processing, composition, and computer music. *ACH* is published in Israel by JAI Press, Inc.

Artificial Intelligence and Music

Antonio Camurri has edited selected proceedings from the European Workshop on Artificial Intelligence and Music (Genoa, 1989) for publication in *Interface* 19(1990)/1-3. Contributions include "A Computer-Based Tutor for Beginning Piano Student" by R.

Dannenburg and colleagues, "An Expert System Prototype for the Study of Musical Segmentation" by Lelio Camilleri and others, "A Many-Sorted Approach to Musical Score Interpretation" by Gianni De Poli and others, and a review article on "The Role of Artificial Intelligence in Music Research" by the editor.

Computer Applications in Music

Deta Davis is drafting a supplement of 2000-3000 citations (through 1989) to her recently published bibliography *Computer Applications in Music*. The supplement is scheduled to be published by A-R Editions, Inc. (Madison, WI) in 1991.

Computers in Music

Helmut Schaffrath is the editor of *Computer in der Musik: Über den Einsatz in Wissenschaft, Komposition, und Pädagogik*. The work was scheduled for publication by Metzler in Stuttgart in September 1990. Its contents include "Sampling und Musik-Analyse" by Ugo Will, "Der Rechner in Notationsforschung und musikalischen Analyse" by Iannos Zannos, "Künstliche neuoronale Netzwerke: Neue Ansätze zur ganzheitlichen Informationsverarbeitung in der Musikforschung" by Marc Leman, two articles on algorithmic composition, two articles on MIDI applications, and a lead article, "Zu Einsatz von Computern in Musikwissenschaft und -pädagogik," by the editor. The price is DM 32 (discounted to DM 27 through December 1990).

IEEE Computer

The July 1991 issue of *IEEE Computer* will examine music applications (composition, synthesis, simulation, and tools for analysis) from a computational standpoint. An audio cassette may be provided with the issue. The editor of this issue is Denis Baggi, Istituto Dalle Molle, Corso Elvezia 36, CH-6900 Lugano, Switzerland.

Interactive Melodic Analysis

Barbara Jesser's Ph.D. thesis (Hochschule für Musik, Essen University, 1989) will be published by Peter Lang, Bern, in 1991 or 1992 under the title *Interaktive Melodieanalyse: Methodik und Anwendung computergestützter Analyseverfahren in Musikethnologie und Volksliedforschung: typologische Untersuchung der Balladensammlung des DVA*. In addition to describing her research on ballads, Jesser reviews theories of similarity, concepts of analysis appropriate to this repertory, and computer approaches to these tasks developed under the direction of Helmut Schaffrath at Essen University.

MIDI for the Atari ST

MIDI and Sound Book for the Atari ST by Bernd Enders and Wolfgang Klemme is available from M&T Books, 501 Galveston Dr., Redwood City, CA 94063. In addition to providing basic information about MIDI, the authors discuss programming for the Atari sound chip and other hardware-related information.

Modelling Music Cognition

Lelio Camilleri is compiling a special issue of the journal *Minds and Machines* (a journal of artificial intelligence, philosophy, and cognitive science) on the theme of modelling musical cognition. Contributors include Jamshed Bharucha, Kemal Ebcioğlu, Jim Kippen, Kate Stevens, Eero Tarasti, and the editor. The volume (2/2) is expected to appear early in 1992. *Minds and Machines* is published by Kluwer Academic Publishers.

Models of Musical Communication and Cognition

Marc Leman is the editor of *Models of Musical Communication and Cognition*, a dedicated issue (18/1-2) of *Interface* (ISSN 0303-3902), which is published by Swets and Zeitlinger B.V. The most substantial articles are Mira Balaban's "The Cross-Fertilization Relationship between Music and Artificial Intelligence," David Cope's "Experiments in Music Intelligence," and Leman's "Symbolic and Subsymbolic Information Processing."

Music and the Personal Computer

Music and the Personal Computer: An Annotated Bibliography by William J. Waters was published by Greenwood Press (ISBN 0-313-26790-1) in 1989. Products for the Amiga, Atari, Commodore, IBM PC, Macintosh, and Tandy computers are discussed.

The Musical Microcomputer

Craig Lister is the author of *The Musical Microcomputer: A Resource Guide* (New York, 1988). The publisher is Garland Press, 136 Madison Avenue, New York, NY 10016.

Pascal Programming for Music Research

Alexander Brinkman's *Pascal Programming for Music Research* (ISBN-0-226-07508-7) has recently been published by the University of Chicago Press. The work provides substantial coverage of Pascal programming in general and selective consideration of music codes (especially SCORE and DARMS) and contemporary analytical applications. The book includes a program library and a large number of illustrations of encodings and analytical results.

Programs of Study

Cogswell College: B. S.
Cogswell Polytechnical College in Cupertino, CA, introduced a B.S. in Music Engineering Technology in 1989. The course work emphasizes signal processing, recording technology, and MIDI applications. Eric Peterson directs the program. Cogswell College is located at 10420 Bubb Road, Cupertino, CA 95014 (408-252-5550),

The Queen's University: M. A.
The Queen's University of Belfast introduced an M.A. in Music and Computing in October 1990. The one-year course is available to students with a first degree in either music or computer science. For the first group it provides an introduction to computer software and for the second an introduction to musicology. Three areas available for detailed study are synthesis and composition, music and artificial intelligence, and historical and analytical research. For further information contact Alan Marsden, Department of Music, The Queen's University, Belfast BT7 1NN, Northern Ireland, UK.

Theses

■ Kemal Ebcioğlu's Ph.D. thesis, "An Expert System for Harmonization of Chorales in the Style of J. S. Bach," is available as Technical Report 86-09 from the Dept. of Computer Science, State University of New York at Buffalo, 226 Bell Hall, Buffalo, NY 14260.

■ Sevan Ficici, in a Master's degree project (Music) at the Eastman School of Music, has been attempting to create non-harmonic tone models for contextual assessment of individual notes in tonal pieces. The programs are in Pascal and run on a Sun workstation. The music (currently Bach chorale harmonizations) is encoded in DARMS and internally represented using Aleck Brinkman's score structure.

■ Simon Holland completed a Ph.D. thesis on "Artificial Intelligence, Education, and Music" at the end of 1989. It is available as Technical Report No. 88 from CITE, The Institute for Educational Technology, The Open University, Milton Keynes, England MK7 6AA.

■ Eric Isaacson (Music) is examining measures (by Forte, Teitelbaum, Morris, Lord, Rahn, Lewin, and the author) of intervallic similarity between pitch-class sets with a view toward showing that the interval content of pitch collections was used by composers to delineate musical structure. He is developing a program in Turbo Pascal that allows users to obtain quickly the value of any measure of similarity applied to any two pitch-class sets. His work is carried out at Indiana University.

■ James Janzen (Music) is seeking to develop a database for folksong classification, retrieval, and analysis at the University of Calgary.

■ Neill Kipp (Computer Science) developed a prototype Standard Music Description Language Processor as his M.S. project at Florida State University in April 1990 [see *Standards* for further information].

■ Christoph Lischka (Mathematics and Computer Science, St. Augustin, Germany), whose long-term objective is the automatic harmonization of Bach chorales, is currently completing a transputer-based implementation of the Boltzmann machine (a specific neural net architecture).

■ R. Wood Massi is currently conducting research for a Ph.D. thesis (Music) on "Computer and Graphic Music: A Semiotic Study of Notation Systems" for submission to the University of California at San Diego. The work concentrates on the ways in which various notations constrain or facilitate musical communication. This consideration extends to languages used in music representation and programming (Music V, DARMS, MIDI, et al.) as well as theories from linguistics, semiotics, cybernetics, and other disciplines.

■ James Rhodes (Computer Science) is developing music-analytical applications within the framework of an expert system, the General System Problem Solver formulated by George J. Klir. Rhodes' specific work concerns the abstract systematic properties of dissonance resolution in four-voice works from the past five centuries. He uses the *Shannon entropy* for the purpose of determining overall consistency of dissonance resolution, and *join procedures* as a means of determining the strength of association among various parts of a musical system. The work was begun as part of a project for the degree of M.Sc. at the State University of New York at Binghamton. GSPS software is available there and at Cornell University.

■ Peer Sitter completed a *Staatsexamensarbeit* entitled "MIDI in der Musikanalyse: Einführung in Theoretische Perspektiven" [MIDI in Musical Analysis: Introduction to Theoretical Perspectives] at the University of Wuppertal in 1988. His work examines the advantages and disadvantages of MIDI code for musicological applications and proposes controller messages to compensate for some of the latter.

■ Janet Owens Thomas is creating a group of programs to generate music algorithmically from fractals as a research project for the M.Sc. in Music Technology at York University.

■ Wolfgang Vonolfen (Mathematics and Computer Science, St. Augustin, Germany) is using neural nets (in Objectworks) to optimize score layout as part of a Ph.D. thesis.

■ Stephen Wu (Computer Science) is working toward the goal of automatic arrangement of popular song melodies. He has been developing a deterministic algorithm for rhythmic segmentation of melodies and plans soon to develop an algorithm for chordal accompaniment. His research is carried out at the University of Hong Kong. Further details are given on p. 115.

Humanities Computing Initiatives and Publications

Computers in Literature

Computers in Literature is the newsletter (ISSN 0958-7381) of the Computers in Teaching Initiative Centre for Literary and Linguistic Studies at Oxford University. It carries brief reports on many activities related to the encoding and processing of academic texts. For further information send a note to CTILIT@VAX.OX.AC.UK.

History and Computing

History and Computing is the new journal of the Association for History and Computing. It is edited by R. J. Morris (Dept. of Economic and Social History, William Robertson Building, George Square, Edinburgh EH8 9JY, Scotland) and published by Oxford University Press. Its areas of concern include quantitative methods, free text analysis, image processing, and graphical presentation.

Humanities Computing Yearbook

The second *Humanities Computing Yearbook*, for 1988, was scheduled for publication by Oxford University Press in 1990. The yearbook provides an annotated survey of current publications, research activities, software, and hardware relevant to humanities teaching and research. The contribution on music was compiled by Lelio Camilleri and Eleanor Selfridge-Field. *HCY 2* is edited by Ian Lancashire at the Center for Computing in the Humanities at the University of Toronto.

Journal of Computer Assisted Learning

The quarterly *Journal of Computer Assisted Learning* is now in its sixth year of publication. The editor is R. Lewis (ESRC, Department of Psychology, University of Lancaster LA1 4YE, UK). *JCAL* considers topics in expert systems, human-computer interfaces, and the psychology of learning in relation to classroom teaching and educational policy. It is available from Blackwell Scientific Publications.

National Center for Machine-Readable Texts

The establishment of a Center for Machine-Readable Texts in the Humanities serving the United States, Canada, and Mexico was discussed at an invited conference jointly sponsored by Rutgers and Princeton Universities in March 1990. Among the Center's functions would be the maintenance of an inventory of machine-readable texts to be made available through the Research Libraries Information Network (RLIN) and the establishment of an archiving service. Eleanor Selfridge-Field was present as a representative of CCARH. There was no discussion of machine-readable musical sources nor of multimedia sources in other disciplines.

Rutgers and Princeton have subsequently agreed to provide start-up funding for the Center. Further information is available from Marianne Gaunt, Associate University Librarian, Rutgers University, New Brunswick, NJ 08903, and Robert Hollander, Director, Italian Studies, Princeton University, Princeton, NJ 08544 (bobh@phoenix. princeton.edu).

Oxford Text Archives

The Oxford Text Archives, founded in 1976, offers long-term storage and maintenance of electronic versions of scholarly texts. Materials may be used for private study only but are easily available for a small fee on diskette, tape, or cartridge, depending on the length of the source and the medium desired. Among items listed in the latest catalogue are the *Oxford Dictionary of Music* (U-592-E), the King James (U-1060-E) and Revised Standard Version (U-1061-E) of the Bible, *Das Nibelungenlied* (U-202-B), and a corpus of Latvian folksong texts (U-287-B). For further information contact Lou Burnard, OTA, 13 Banbury Road, Oxford OX2 6NN (archive@vax.ox.ac.uk).

Oxford Text Searching System

The Oxford Text Searching System is designed to make set texts for undergraduate study in English, ancient, medieval, and modern languages and literature, and theology available for online searching. It is associated with the newly formed Centre for Humanities Computing. The texts used are principally those held by the Oxford Text Archives [see above]. Software support for searching and for the preparation of concordances and indices is available. Enquiries may be directed to Susan Hockey (SUSAN@VAX.AC.UK).

Scholarship and Technology in the Humanities

An invited international conference on Scholarship and Technology in the Humanities, convened by J. M. Smedhurst, head of the British Library, was held at Elvetham Hall, UK, from May 9 through 12. Consideration of the prospects for each discipline over the next decade was given in a series of prepared talks. Walter B. Hewlett represented the Center for Computer Assisted Research in the Humanities.

Special Topics

Encoding Neumes and Mensural Notation

The term *neumes* encompasses a broad range of notational phenomena in medieval and Renaissance music. From a representational viewpoint, medieval neumes normally preserve pitch information but lack either durational information or a secure basis on which to interpret it. Pitches may be joined in *ligatures* that assume a range of composite shapes. In mensural notation rhythmic indications are more highly evolved but complex. The coloration of neumes and the tempus and prolation signs at the start of a piece must be correctly observed to produce an accurate modern transcription.

The representation of neumes has been accomplished in various ways, usually in a way tailored to the representation of one particular repertory. Yet a sufficient number of dedicated solutions has accrued to provide some basis for a broadened view of the subject. As a supplement to our 1987 review article on music representation, we have collected available information on existing approaches to the encoding of neumes.

As in other contexts, the best choices for encoding methods must be made with due regard for both the nature of the original material and the purposes for which the machine-readable code will be used. Works may be encoded for printing, for analysis, and for long-term storage leading to multiple uses, in which case completeness of information is highly desirable. Much work on medieval chant has relied on numerical or letter-name encoding of pitches to create indices and concordances. The Bryden and Hughes *Index to Gregorian Chant* (Harvard University Press, 1969) is illustrative. It contains pitch encodings of 11,000 chant incipits. More recent work by Andrew Hughes and Richard Crocker proceeds along similar lines, although towards different goals.

A common goal of studies of monophonic repertories is to trace the transmission of melodic formulae and patterns with a view towards establishing chronological sequence, geographical spread, and paths of greatest influence. *Centonization* is a term borrowed from studies of the epic to describe the processes of melodic absorption and accretion that occurred in the oral transmission of chant repertories. *Attribute description* is often a necessary first step toward describing the general properties of a repertory. The absence of reliable means of rhythmic interpretation for many early repertories suggests an area in which the computer may eventually come to play an important role in testing diverse hypotheses.

Monophonic Repertories

A long-held view of the development of European medieval music is that monophonic pieces were originally set with one note to a syllable and that as time passed it became common to set some syllables of text with a few notes and eventually to set highly significant words, such as *alleluia*, with long melismas. The theory is losing ground as an oversimplified and in many cases inaccurate one, but it is helpful in understanding the development of musical notation. Ligatures came about in order to accommodate the *neumatic* setting of multiple notes to one syllable of text.

In modern transcription, monophonic repertories are now easily encoded by many program for music printing. The earliest computational studies of medieval music, which date back to the 1960's, considerably predate the advent of this modern convenience. Among the early computer-assisted studies of medieval repertories was that of Raymond Erickson on thirteenth-century rhythm ("Rhythmic Problems and Melodic Structure in *Organum Purum*: A Computational Study," Ph.D. thesis, Yale University, 1970). A number of studies of medieval music were prepared under the direction of Ian Bent and John Morehen, in particular at Nottingham University over the past two decades. DARMS, which provides for the complete encoding of musical notation, has been the language of choice in most of these studies. A more limited numerical system of representation was used in David Halperin's two theses on troubadour music (1978) and Ambrosian chant (1986), both completed at Tel-Aviv University. Until recently encodings of medieval music were based on modern editions of the repertory.

The task of interest for present purposes is to encode directly from the source in such a way as to preserve information about the original presentation of the musical information provided and to avoid forced interpretations of notational elements of uncertain meaning. The systems cited below, which originated between the mid-1970's and late 1980's, all attempt in various ways to address that goal.

Leo J. Plenckers at Amsterdam University has successfully encoded the *Cantigas de Santa Maria* from a modern edition using a self-designed system of representation. To capture information about the shapes of neumes, ligatures, and complexes, Plenckers developed alphabetic codes suggested by the shapes of the symbols. Connected neumes and ligatures were formed by combinations of these:

The letter *o* = *obliqua*. If the second note is higher than the first, an *h* immediately follows the hyphen; if it is left-facing, an *l* is placed after the appropriate letter. Complexes involving longer strings of these encodings are joined by the sign "+".

Plenckers was able to write a grammar for parsing the encoded songs into elements and to facilitate pattern matching. He then explored questions of pattern formation and drew attention to similarities between Algerian songs and items in this thirteenth-century repertory. The details of the system and some of the analytic results are reported in Plenckers' article "Pattern Recognition in the Study of the *Cantigas de Santa Maria*" (*Musical Grammars and Computer Analysis*, ed. Mario Baroni and Laura Callegari, Florence, 1984, pp. 59-70). The fact that the author was able to use the information analytically attests its practical value.

The SCRIBE system developed by John Stinson, John Griffiths, and Brian Parish at La Trobe and Melbourne Universities in Australia has been used in the encoding of approximately 3000 monophonic works (ballades, caccie, lays, virelais, rondeaux, *et al*.) from the fourteenth century. The latest version of the support software facilitates the encoding of approximately 20 neume shapes. Searches for neume types may be conducted. Analytical work with this repertory has extended to contour comparisons with chant from earlier centuries, including the tenth, for which striking resemblances have been found in the fourteenth-century material. There is now a capability to produce round stemless noteheads with slurs indicating the ligatures of the square notation. Two- and three-note ligatures have codes derived from chant nomenclature: Pd = *podatus*, Pr = *porrectus*, etc. The codes currently in use are these:

Below we see a SCRIBE transcription [in black neumes on a staff of six red lines] of the tenor of Landini's ballata "Gia ebbi libertate" and the source on which it is based:

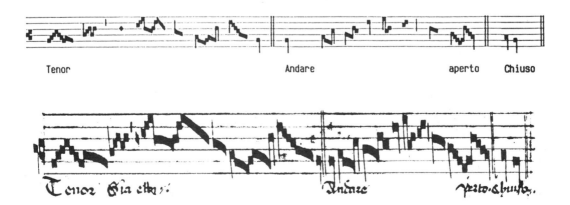

In a dissertation study currently underway, Hilde Binford-Walsh at Stanford University is using *SCORE* to encode Aquitainian chant. Her interest is in establishing a melodic grammar. She encodes both neume shapes and absolute values and performs numerous statistical tests on the resulting data.

The work of Catherine Harbor and Andy Reid at Royal Holloway and Bedford New College in the UK on a program called *PLAINSONG* is devoted to the entry and use of black neumatic notation on a four-line stave. The range of neume forms provided supports work with both printed and manuscript repertories. There is also a facility for entering episemata [strokes added to neumes to denote elongation] of varying lengths either above or below the neumes, as appropriate. Printing capabilities are discussed on p. 70.

PLAINSONG includes two analytic modules, both of which can operate at varying levels of detail. A variant module compares up to 30 versions of a chant against a master version and prints each item in schematic form, with or without text underlay, under the master. A similarity search module compares a given chant quotation with a series of materials in files specified by the researcher and reports potential matches. Comparisons of neumes, text, melody, and episemata are all supported. Further information is available from Catherine Harbor, Computer Centre, Royal Holloway and Bedford New College, Egham Hill, Egham, Surrey TW20 0EX, UK (C.Harbor@vax.rhbnc.ac.uk).

Polyphonic Repertories

Mensural notation defined durational relationships on two levels—that of *tempus*, the basic beat, and that of *prolation*, the number of subdivisions within the beat. Modern 12/8 time could be said to have a tempus of 4 and a prolation of 3. Because of the tiered nature of this system, the graphic image of a note did not fully define its value. That had to be computed with reference to tempus and prolation signs given at the start of a work. Various systems were devised to express more clearly the appropriate relationships. In white mensural notation, noteheads could be filled or void. In more elaborate systems, red notes (either filled or void) could be used in conjunction with black notes (either filled or void). The invention of dots of addition in the early sixteenth century led to the gradual decline of mensural notation. Much of the music of the preceding, highly illustrious decades is preserved in mensural notation. The idea of mensuration lingered in the "colored" notation of the seventeenth century. Filled whole notes and void eighth notes occurred in passages which contradicted the accentuation scheme suggested by the meter signature [an example is shown on p. 103].

Considerable attention has been devoted to the encoding of mensural notation. Norbert Böker-Heil's work on the Renaissance *Tenorlied*, resulting in a three-volume edition (Kassel: Bärenreiter, 1979-86), involved the encoding and printing of mensural notation and provided extensive support for its analysis [see the 1988 *Directory*, pp. 122-125]. A provision for sound output has subsequently been added.

Tom Hall's *FASTCODE* was in use at Princeton University in the 1970's and early 80's to encode white mensural notation of the fifteenth and sixteenth centuries, particularly in the works of Josquin and Lassus. Hall's system supported note values from the *semifusa* (the equivalent of sixteenth notes) through the perfect *maxima* (the equivalent of twelve semibreves) and could accommodate time changes local to one voice.

Other programs with the ability to print mensural notation include *SCRIBE, SCORE, Subtilior Press, WOLFGANG,* and *ALPHA/TIMES. Subtilior* [shown in 1989] creates an electronic facsimile rather than an actual encoding of the source. *ALPHA/TIMES* can produce a facsimile [p. 35] but it supports encoding and searching. These two programs run on the Macintosh. *SCRIBE* is oriented more toward storage and retrieval of information [described above] than towards printing of mensural notation, but its two-color plotter output makes a very attractive facsimile. *SCORE* and *WOLFGANG* both provide both facsimile and modern notation options for mensural notation together with complete encoding. [An example from a preliminary version of *WOLFGANG* is shown on p. 35.] The three last-named programs run on the IBM PC.

Many kinds of historical and analytical research on repertories of the Renaissance require, in addition to an adequate code for the symbols encountered in the source, an articulate understanding of implied durational differences between elements that are graphically the same. One carefully rationalized approach to the encoding of mensural notation that exhibits this important quality was devised by Lynn Trowbridge as a set of extensions to DARMS for thesis research carried out at the University of Illinois in the late 1970's. We are reproducing here, with the author's permission, the salient points of this system because they are of potentially broad applicability to other projects.

Trowbridge's *Linear Music Input Language* for Analysis

Trowbridge's immediate task was the encoding for a large repertory of fifteenth-century chansons. The *Linear Music Input Language* (1980) that he used to encode this repertory is a modified subset of DARMS that facilitates dealing with the durational complexities of the music. The logic underlying his system could fruitfully be applied to the encoding of any repertory with the same characteristics. While we cannot fully reproduce the manual here, we should like to call attention to some general elements of the approach.

Voices. In specifying the voice part being encoded, Trowbridge specified the total number of voices in the work. He differentiates between a *Cantus Superius* in a two-voice texture, a *Cantus* in a three-voice texture, a *Cantus* in a four-voice texture, and a *Superius* in a five-voice work. Although this is irrelevant to representation *per se*, it has enviable strengths for analytical studies.

Staff placement codes follow customary DARMS practice. The bottom line of any staff is "1"; DARMS has no true pitch code. Clef codes, preceded by an exclamation mark, are formed by coupling the line number with the sign C, F, or G (!3G, !7C). In key codes (introduced as !K), a flat is a minus (-) and a sharp is a plus (+), and a numeral indicates the number of pitch classes affected. !K1- introduces a work with one flat.

Meter involves two variables—tempus and prolation. Perfect (triple) tempus was expressed by a circle, imperfect (duple) tempus by a C (understood to be an incomplete circle). Numerals were used for perfect (3) and imperfect (2) prolation.

In Trowbridge's system, the representation of tempus and prolation is treated as if the music were in modern notation. The following meter codes are employed:

$\frac{2}{4}$	C	2:4		$\frac{6}{4}$	φ, C3	6:4
$\frac{3}{4}$	O	3:4		$\frac{9}{4}$	O3	9:4
$\frac{2}{2}$	C2, ¢, Ɔ	2:2		$\frac{6}{8}$	ℭ	6:8
$\frac{3}{2}$	O2	3:2		$\frac{9}{8}$	⊙	9:8

Composite examples of the encoding of clef, key, and meter signatures are as follows:

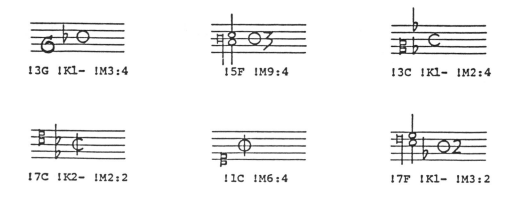

!3G !K1- !M3:4   !5F !M9:4   !3C !K1- !M2:4

!7C !K2- !M2:2   !1C !M6:4   !7F !K1- !M3:2

It is one thing to have such coding tools available but quite another to interpret the music correctly in each metrical context. To address this problem, Trowbridge developed a table of codes (W = whole, H = half, Q = quarter, etc.) to be used for each durational species in relation to the original note shape (fusa, semiminim, etc.) in each respective meter. In this table Dot. = dotted, Per. = perfect, Imp. = imperfect, and Col. = colored.

Note shapes	2/4 C	3/4 O	2/2 ¢ C2 Ɔ	3/2 O2	6/4 φ C3	9/4 O3	6/8 Ȼ	9/8 ⊙
Fusa	T	T	T	T	T	T	T	T
Semiminim	S	S	S	S	S	S	S	S
Dot. semiminim	S.	S.	S.	S.	S.	S.	S.	S.
Col. minim	&2/3 E*	E	&2/3 E*	&2/3 E*	E	E		
Col. min. (+ SBr)	S	S	S	S	S	S		
Minim	E	E	E	E	E	E	E	E
Dot. minim	E.	E.	E.	E.	E.	E.	E.	E.
Col. semibreve	&2/3 Q*	Q	&2/3 Q*	&2/3 Q*	Q	Q	Q	Q
Col. SBr (+ min.)	E.	E.	E.	E.	E.	E.		
Imp. semibreve	Q	Q	Q	Q	Q	Q	Q	Q
Per. semibreve							Q.	Q.
Dot. semibreve	Q.	Q.	Q.	Q.	Q.	Q.		
Col. breve	&2/3 H*	H	&2/3 H*	&2/3 H*	H	H		H
Imp. breve	H	H	H	H	H	H	H.	H.
Per. breve		H.			H.	H.		WJE
Dot. breve	H.		H.	H.				
Col. long	&2/3 W*	W	&2/3 W*	W	W	W.		
Imp. long	W	W.	W	W	W.	W.	W.	BJQ
Per. long				W.		BJQ		
Dot. long	W.	BJQ	W.		BJQ		BJQ	B.JQJE
Imp. maxima	B	B.	B	B.	B.	B.JWJH	B.	B.JWJH

By using three units to represent the smallest note encountered, Trowbridge avoided fractional parts in the representation of colored (e.g. triplet) notes. The numerical value of each note is shown in the following table:

Note shapes	2/4 C	3/4 O	2/2 ¢ C2 ⊃	3/2 O2	6/4 φ C3	9/4 O3	6/8 ₵	9/8 O
Fusa	3	3	3	3	3	3	3	3
Semiminim	6	6	6	6	6	6	6	6
Dot. semiminim	9	9	9	9	9	9	9	9
Col. minim	8	12	8	8	12	12		
Col. minim (+ semibreve)	6	6	6	6	6	6		
Minim	12	12	12	12	12	12	12	12
Dot. minim	18	18	18	18	18	18	18	18
Col. semibreve	16	24	16	16	24	24	24	24
Col. semibreve (+ minim)	18	18	18	18	18	18		
Imp. semibreve	24	24	24	24	24	24	24	24
Per. semibreve							36	36
Dot. semibreve	36	36	36	36	36	36		
Col. breve	32	48	32	32	48	48		72
Imp. breve	48	48	48	48	48	48	72	72
Per. breve		72			72	72		108
Dot. breve	72		72	72				
Col. long	64	96	64	96	96	144		
Imp. long	96	144	96	96	144	144	144	216
Per. long				144		216		
Dot. long	144	216	144		216		216	324
Imp. maxima	192	288	192	288	288	432	288	432

Each possible numeric representation appears once in the following summary table:

LMIL code	Proportional representation	Note shapes			
		Perfect	Imperfect	Colored	Modern
T	3				
S	6				
&2/3 E*	8				
S.	9				
E	12				
&2/3 Q*	16				
E.	18				
Q	24				
&2/3 H*	32				
Q.	36				
H	48				
&2/3 W*	64				
H.	72				
W	96				
WJE	108				
W.	144				
B	192				
BJQ	216				
B.	288				
B.JQJE	324				
B.JWJH	432				

Another area of difficulty that Trowbridge resolved is the encoding of non-equivalent rhythmic groupings, such as triplets. Such a group is introduced by an ampersand (&). A reduced fraction in which the numerator indicates the number of rhythmic units actually occupied and the denominator the number of rhythmic units actually specified is employed. The pitch and rhythm codes (disregarding coloration) are then given for each member of the group. An asterisk (*) closes the encoding. Some examples follow.

&2/3 2H 3Q* 4H   &4/5 2S 3 4 2 3* 2Q

&2/3 7H 6E 5* 3Q 4   &2/3 2S 1 2 3 2 1* 2E 3

&2/3 4W 6Q 5*   &4/7 2E 3 4 5 6 7 8*

&2/3 9Q 8 7*   &2/3 2E 3 4 3Q 2E*

This system allows the exact rhythmic value of each member to be obtained by multiplication of the value of each unadjusted rhythmic symbol in the group by the reduced fraction described above.

The solutions to some common problems encountered in the encoding of white mensural notation are indicated in the following encoding, which is interleaved with a transcription of the source:

!3C !K1- !M3:47Q 7 9E. 8T 7 8Q 7E 6 5Q 4 RE 5 4 6E. 7S 8E 7 8 9Q

!1C !M2:2   5W 6 &2/3 7H 6E 5* 4Q 7 6 5H 4Q 5H RQ 5 9Q. 8S 7 6H

!7C !K1- !M3:47Q. 6E 8 9 30Q. 9S 8 9E. 8S 30Q RE 7 8 7 5S 3 4E 3H

!3C !M3:4   RW. RW. 3Q. 4E 5Q 4 7E. 6S 5Q 4H. 3H 1E 2

!7F !K1- !M3:48H 8Q 8 7 8E 5 8Q 5E 7Q 8E 5Q RQ 1

The complete LMIL manual is contained in Trowbridge's thesis, *The Fifteenth-Century French Chanson: A Computer-Aided Study of Styles and Style Change* (University of Illinois, 1982), UMI #8209635, pp. 275-89. An abridged version of his findings was published as "Style Change in the Fifteenth-Century Chanson" in the *Journal of Musicology*, IV/2 (1985-6), 146-70.

Printing Mensural Notation

From systems that support the printing of mensural notation [see pp. 26-7 above], we provide a few examples of developments over the past ten years.

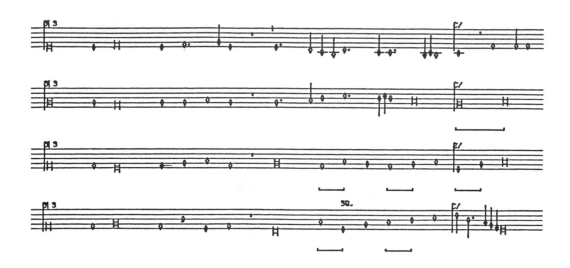

White mensural notation in score from Josquin's "Planxit autem David," produced via plotter by Tom Hall's FASTCODE, *c*. 1981. In this example, a change from Ꝺ3 to ₵ is represented. "SQ." indicated two square neumes, as opposed to one *obliqua*, in the original source.

Red [here grey] and black mensural notation produced with a pen plotter by SCRIBE *c*. 1988. Note shapes can be represented as black, red, void, or red-void.

Kyrie. Fons bonitatis pater ingenite

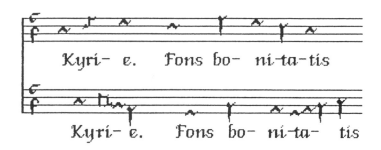

Transcription of polyphonic manuscript (St. Gall) showing neumes on four-line staves produced by Christoph Schnell's ALPHA/TIMES *c.* 1987.

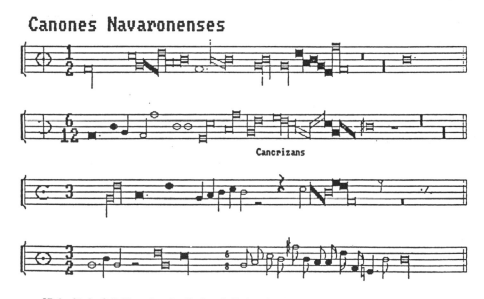

Set of canons with complex mensural relationships produced by Etienne Darbellay's WOLFGANG *c.* 1986. See also p. 103.

Optical Recognition of Musical Data

There are several approaches to optical recognition of musical data, a topic that *Computing in Musicology* has followed for several years. Intelligent recognition of musical information must be distinguished from the capture of bit-mapped images as graphics information only. Intelligently scanned data can be manipulated and channeled to formats and uses different from the original one. In principle, optical recognition of musical data builds on the foundation of text scanning procedures. In text each character has a single identity and the number of characters is finite. Except in ligatures, characters appear as separate entities. Their meaning is the same, regardless of the context. The exact formation and size of an individual character varies from font to font, however, and many hundreds of fonts are encountered.

A simple approach to character recognition of both alphabetic text and of musical text is that of *template-matching*. The templates are based on particular fonts. Recognition programs are easily confused by graphic input that varies from font-specific descriptions in memory. This suggests that they are serviceable in situations where the material at hand is self-consistent but limited in value for handling typographically diverse materials.

A contrasting approach is that of *geometrical analysis* of graphic features such as lines, angles, orientations, and curvatures of scanned objects. Recognition is based on algorithmic matching. This approach overcomes the problems of exactness encountered in template-matching but elicits new areas of confusion in attempting to distinguish, for example, between b's and h's, l's and 1's, or O's and 0's. These kinds of misreadings are so subtle that they are difficult to detect in proofreading. Uncorrected errors can lead to bizarre results in processing of data.

The optical scanning of music cannot build entirely on these approaches, because the symbols used in musical notation are so much more numerous, their visual grammar so much more complex, and their meanings sometimes determined by contextual clues. Even the question of what constitutes an object is confusing. A single pitch is a discrete sound object. Its representation can comprise several graphics objects such as a notehead, a stem, and a flag or beam, for example. An isolated notehead means little as a "recognized" object, because from it we cannot determine pitch without intelligent information about a preceding clef sign and staff position, nor can we determine duration without information about its coloration, its stem (if any), and any possible flags.

To overcome these problems, researchers have explored the technique of *bounding* groups of objects, such as a series of eighth notes connected to a common beam, and defining the contents hierarchically from most to least comprehensive. The demarcated area is called a bounding box. They have explored foreground-background separation (i.e., removing the staff lines to expose the notes), background enhancement, tests of identity by rotation and/or slanting of objects, and a host of other image-processing techniques. Since the automatic recognition of the 26 characters of the Roman alphabet is still an imperfect art, we do not anticipate a fully accurate technique of automatic recognition of musical information soon. Yet activity in this area of research has significantly increased in the past year, and the various approaches employed will undoubtedly be of value in clarifying the circumstances under which different procedures are most appropriate. We offer below reports from several groups and individuals working in this area.

University of Surrey/OUP

The work of Nicholas Carter, R. A. Bacon, and T. Messenger at the University of Surrey in Guildford, England, is firmly focused on the acquisition of printed music in common musical notation. The project is sponsored by Oxford University Press.

The work is conducted in a hybrid environment of UNIX and DOS. Development of the recognition software takes place under UNIX on a Sun386i workstation. Input is via a Hewlett Packard ScanJet flatbed scanner interfaced with the workstation. Output is in the form of a file compatible with the SCORE music publishing program, which operates under DOSWindows on the Sun386i. [Sample input and output were shown in last year's issue of *CM*, pp. 32-3.]

Currently a wide range of models for use in the recognition process is being constructed. A provisional vocabulary of symbols is to be devised from the first volume of the complete works of C. P. E. Bach (Vol. 24, Ser. I, containing solo keyboard music), which was brought out recently by OUP. The contents have been divided into a training data set and a test data set. The aim of the work is to enable conversion of existing printed music into machine-readable form, thus enabling applications such as electronic publishing, computer-based editing, musicological analysis, and automatic production of Braille music.

Among publications relating to this project are Carter's Ph.D. thesis, "Automatic Recognition of Printed Music in the Context of Electronic Publishing," which was completed at the University of Surrey in 1989, and "Automatic Recognition of Music Notation" by Carter and Bacon in the pre-*Proceedings of the International Association for Pattern Recognition Workshop on Syntactic and Structural Pattern Recognition* (Murray Hill, NJ, June 1990), 482.

University of Wales/Cardiff

The work on optical character recognition for printed music notation that has been in progress for three years at the University of Wales College of Cardiff is based on an IBM PC AT and uses an IBM 3117 flatbed scanner. One of the particular objectives is to develop a low-cost system that might be affordable to small printing companies or individual musicians. The overall objectives are otherwise the same as those described above.

Much of the research has concentrated on finding computationally efficient methods of determining the identities of each musical symbol. The recognition of single-line melodies now approaches 95% accuracy. More complicated examples involving chords have an accuracy rate between 80% and 95%.

A current focus is on contiguous objects, such as the noteheads shown in the accompanying illustration. The printout of the results of the program is an ordered list of the musical objects that have been identified. The order is by the sequence in which the symbols appear from left to right in the music. The only error in this example is that four of the staccato dots were ignored by the system. The duration column computes the number of sixteenth notes involved.

This research has been undertaken for a Ph.D. thesis that, it is anticipated, will be completed before the end of 1990. The project will continue at least until September 1992.

Music to be scanned by the Cardiff program:

Stage I—Removal of staff lines

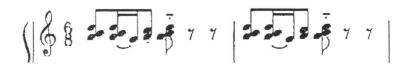

Stage II—File listing of scanned objects:

Symbol Identity	Duration	Horizontal Position	Pitch of Note or Symbol		
Barline		55			
Clef		83			
Time Signature		122			
S Beamed Group	2	177	d'	a	b
B Slur		218			
Beamed Group	1	220	d'	a	b
E Slur		245			
Beamed Group	1	251	g		
Dot		278	f		
F Beamed Group	2	278	c'	a	
Note	2	312	a	d'	b
Tenuto		320			
Dot		320	g'		
Rest	2	360			
Rest	2	403			
Barline		443			
S Beamed Group	2	477	d'	a	b
B Slur		517			
Beamed Group	1	518	d'	a	b
E Slur		545			
Beamed Group	1	551	g		
F Beamed Group	2	578	c'	a	
Note	2	613	a	d'	b
Dot		620	g'		
Tenuto		621			
Rest	2	659			
Rest	2	703			
Barline		742			

```
Bar 0 -  0 beats
Bar 1 - 12 beats
Bar 2 - 12 beats
```

Note that staccato dots are given a pitch value to represent their placement on the staff. Note also the processing order of the graphic elements in the different presentations of the a-b-d' chord.

Waseda University

An automated recognition system for reading musical scores forms part of Waseda University's "Music and Vision" research program, a fundamental tenet of which is that visual aspects of music are of comparable informational importance with acoustic aspects of music. The automated recognition of notated music relies on a computer vision technique. The illustrations following show several stages in the recognition process. Note that in this approach staff lines are added to clarify placement. The reading time for a commercially available nursery song with three real voices is about 10 seconds. Once the data acquisition has been performed, wider applications are possible in the fields of computer music and music information processing.

The musician robot WABOT-2, developed at Waseda University, reads a musical score in real time and plays the electronic organ with its ten fingers. [Scanned music from this system was shown in the 1986 issue, p. 34]. The principal source on WABOT is S. Ohteru et al., "Automated High Speed Recognition of Printed Music" in the *Proceedings of the International Conference on Advanced Robotics* (1985), 482-577.

Other facets of research by this group, which includes Takebumi Itagaki and Masayuki Isogai as well as Sadamu Ohteru at Waseda University and Shuji Hashimoto at Toho University, are a bilateral translation system to facilitate conversion between printed and Braille music and automatic recognition of dance patterns in real time. In the latter case a data base of choreographies is under development through a program for automatic recognition of dance notation. [For information on dance notation software, see pp. 107-11.] *Standard Music Expression (SMX)*, one of the representation schemes used in this research, was shown in the 1987 *Directory*, pp. 16-7.

(a) Original music:

(b) Normalized picture:

(c) Determination of notehead locations against an expanded staff:

(d) Individual symbols captured:

(e) Output of score data after analysis:

Musical Interval	C0	C2	C0	BA	B9	BA	C0		B7	B9	BA		B9	BA	C0
Sound Type	01	01	02	02	02	02	04		02	02	04		02	02	04
Sound Duration	12	06	0C	0C	0C	0C	18		0C	0C	18		0C	0C	18

Intervals: in the left column, A, B, and C are octave designations. In the right column, pitches are represented as chromatic units in hexadecimal notation. Numeric 0 = pitch 0 = C, irrespective of tonality. Numeric A = pitch 10 = B♭ and numeric B = pitch 11 = B♮.

Sound types: 1 = unaccented, 2 = staccato, 4 = tenuto.

Sound durations: these are indicated in two-digit hexadecimal notation, from which rhythmic relationships can be deduced. Hex 6 = decimal 6, hex 12 = decimal 18, hex 0C = decimal 12.

University of Ottawa

At the University of Ottawa, William McGee and Paul Merkley have been engaged both in research on optical scanning and on uncovering the many layers in the process of the transformation from cheironomic to diastematic notation in medieval music. The broad aim is to provide a fast, error-free method of entering musical samples into a format that permits statistical analysis, string searches, editing, and printing on IBM PC compatibles. Although this account concentrates on their work with medieval manuscripts, the research extends to common notation from printed sources.

Cheironomic notation, which is thought to have originated in the eighth century, is not pitch-specific. It tells the reader only whether the next note is higher or lower and with what vocal nuance it should be sung. It is believed that the singers for whom this chant was intended were already familiar with the basic melodies, which were transmitted orally, and that the notation was merely a stimulus to correct performance.

In later *diastematic notation*, pitch is specified but there is little allowance for the expression of nuance. Its function was to preserve and aid in the transmission of the repertory. Although the neumes it used were originally unlined, colored and dry-point lines were added gradually and by the eleventh century clefs and staves had come into regular use. The forms of individual neumes changed as the background developed.

To develop a scanning system for early medieval music, the Ottawa researchers began with lined notation of chant with neumes in square notation, which presents few difficulties of syntax. They first remove the lines. The quality and distortion of the material are such that this procedure involves sampling a number of positions along presumed lines. For the interpretation of individual neumes, pattern recognition and thin-line coding procedures have both been explored. Through vertical and horizontal assessment based on the latter, square neumes can be detected by their resemblance to their counterparts in cheironomic notation. Bounding boxes are used to create a dynamic dictionary of neume shapes; the dictionary facilitates component identification, which involves pattern-matching procedures.

The original scanning is done with a Hewlett Packard Scanjet flatbed scanner interfaced to an IBM PC XT computer. Interpreted output is converted to a DARMS file and printed with *The Note Processor*. Research on the scanning of music in common musical notation is also in progress.

The materials shown on the following page were scanned from *Paléographie musicale* (Tournai, 1889--) materials relating to the "Justus ut palma florebit" family, a text cycle set to different melodies. Paul Merkley, who provided this information, is the author of *Italian Tonaries* (Ottawa, 1988) and "Tonaries and Melodic Families of Antiphons," *Journal of the Plainsong and Medieval Music Society* (1989).

(a) Original image:

(b) Image corrected by straightening staff lines:

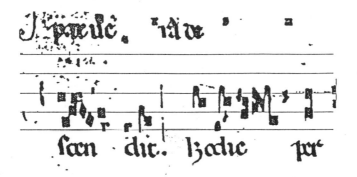

(c) Image with staff lines and other visual irrelevancies removed:

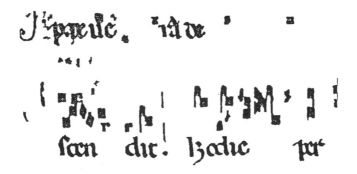

Three stages in the scanning of medieval music.

ERATTO-C.N.R.S./Paris

The focus of research into optical scanning by Dimitris Giannelos at ERATTO, a part of the Centre National de Recherche Scientifique in Paris, is concerned with capturing the graphic symbols of traditional Greek Orthodox sacred music from printed sources. His programs, for which he currently claims an accuracy rate of 80%, run on the Macintosh Plus. A version for the IBM PC is in preparation. The program will be made commercially available. Data can also be used analytically. Transcription has been fully automatic since June 1989. Output is channeled through Michel Wallet's *Euterpe* [see *Software for Music Printing*] to a laser printer.

ΜΑΚΑΡΙΟΣ   ΑΝΗΡ

Πέτρου Λαμπαδαρίου τοῦ Πελοποννησίου (+1777)
συντμηθὲν ὑπὸ Μανουὴλ Πρωτοψάλτου (+1819)

ᵉΗχος ᾱ ᾆ Νη

Ma κα   ρι ι   ο ος α α νηρ ο   ος ϩ ϩκ ε   πο ρε   ε ευ   θη η   εν

βϩ λη   η   η   α   α σε   ε   εβων ᾇκαι εν   ο   δω ω   α α μαρ τω

λω ων ϩ ϩκ   ε   ε ε   ςη   η ᾇ   και   ε   πι   ι   κα α   θε   ε   ε   δρα α λοι

οι μων   ϩ   ϩκ   ε   ε   κα θη η σε   ε   εν   α αλ λη   η   λϩ   ϩ   ι   ι ι ι   α   ᾇ

Approximate translation: "Blessed [is the] Man [by] Peter Lampadarios of the Peloponnesus arranged and abridged by Manuel Protophaltos" [a leading Greek composer of the fifteenth century]. The text for this "Sequence of the Evening" is taken from Psalm 1 and begins: "Blessed is the man who has not walked in the assembly of the impious and has not stood in the road of sinners and has not sat in the seat of the pernicious. Alleluia."

ΚΟΙΝΩΝΙΚΟΝ

Ἰωάννου τοῦ Κλαδᾶ (ΙΔ΄ καὶ ΙΕ΄ αἰῶνος)

Ἦχος α΄ ἐκ τοῦ Κε

Approximate translation: "[Chant for] Communion [by] John [the son] of Klada" [a leading Greek composer of the late fourteenth century]. Stanza 1 of 25: "Take part, taste, and see that Christ the Lord...."

Computer Enhancement of Paleographic Information

Joan S. Reis, a recently retired member of the Department of Music at the University of Cincinnati and a part-time member of the staff of the Cincinnati Art Museum, has recently raised an interesting question about the use of computer enhancement in paleographic studies.   Her interest came about in an effort to demonstrate that a Gainsborough portrait acquired by the Museum in 1983, as part of the bequest of Agnes S. and Murray Seasongood, is not that of Surgeon-General David Middleton, as supposed for most of the current century, nor of Benjamin Franklin, as supposed for much of the last, but rather an unfinished portrait of Johann Christian Bach, showing him ravaged by tuberculosis near the end of his life.   Bach was living in London when he died early in 1782. Thomas Gainsborough was a personal friend who had twice previously painted his portrait.

Several kinds of evidence are cited in Reis's article "A Third Gainsborough Portrait of Johann Christian Bach?" in *The Musical Quarterly* 74/2 (1990), 295-302. After the frame was removed, Elizabeth Bachelor, Assistant Director of the Museum, requested an infrared scan of the painting.   Infrared reflectography, in which rays pass through the fabric, reveals details of the sub-surface. The image produced may be photographed from a monitor, producing a grainy effect and distorted edges. In this case the scan revealed some hidden writing in the upper left-hand corner. The representation below was made from a black-and-white photograph provided by Reis.

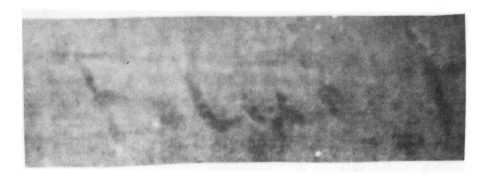

The name "Bach" before enhancement.

From an enlarged print of the negative, it was possible to make out, under paint previously covered by the frame, the letters "Ba ch". In the intervening space an enlarged thread gave the appearance of an "L". The letters are thought to have been separated to accommodate the thread. To differentiate between the thread, which had become darkened with time, and the letters transcribed, and to subdue the background, Jeffry B. Weidner of Xenas Communications in Cincinnati produced the computer enhancement shown below. This provides one of the pieces of evidence cited by Reis.

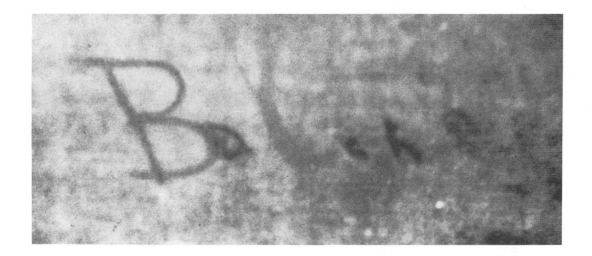

The name "Bach" in an infrared photographic enlargement after computer enhancement.

Our effort at reproducing this material further distorts the original graphic information and is conducive to an uncertain result. Those with a serious interest in the matter should consult evidence closer to the source. We offer the material to call attention to the potential value of such techniques in paleographical studies of all kinds. The portrait is shown on the following page by kind permission of the Cincinnati Art Museum.

A portrait by Thomas Gainsborough recently said by Joan S. Reis to be made of J. C. Bach in *c.* 1781. Used by permission of the Cincinnati Art Museum.

Technical Standards

Technical Standards

Technical standards facilitate the transport of data from one environment to another. The detailed way in which they do this is normally invisible to the user. The complexity of music as a system of information makes the task of standards design arduous. There is a temptation to ignore what is difficult, especially if it is little used in commercial applications. In their role as computer users scholars need not be concerned with the details of standards implementations, but scholars are well qualified to judge the adequacy of proposed standards and are urged to report any concerns they have to the appropriate bodies.

MIDI File Format: Proposed Extensions for Representing Digital Sound

The MIDI (Musical Instrumental Digital Interface) standard was developed to enable communications between electronic instruments and microcomputers. The Standard MIDI File format (ANSI X3V1.8M/88-6), developed in large part by Dave Oppenheim, was adopted in 1987. A description is available electronically from archive-server@bartok. sun.com and in hardcopy from the International MIDI Association, 5316 W. 57th St., Los Angeles, CA 90056.

The musical information that MIDI input can capture is limited to pitch and duration. The sophistication of musical information in the classical repertory is significantly greater that the signal-based information that MIDI interprets. This puts the impetus for refinement on the software developer.

In particular the information required to print music efficiently greatly exceeds what MIDI provides, both quantitatively and qualitatively. Kjell E. Nordli of the Department of Informatics at the University of Norway has proposed that MIDI Files could become a powerful "language" for a more general description of notated music if these files were extended to include certain kinds of additional information. His proposal includes extensions in several areas. We provide here representative items from selected lists.

Enharmonics
The Standard might be extended to provide for optional enharmonic specification in cases in which the sounding note is ambiguous (F#/Gb). The code "xx" indicates the start of such a meta-event. Where "sf" equals an enharmonic specification, the proposed extensions are:

sf = 0: sharp
sf = 1: flat
sf = 2: double sharp
sf = 3: double flat
sf = 4: natural

Dynamics

The code "cc" introduces the following dynamics meta-events:

cc = 0: start of crescendo
cc = 1: end of crescendo
cc = 2: start of decrescendo
cc = 3: end of decrescendo

Accents

The code "aa" introduces the following accents (incomplete list):

aa = 1: tenuto	aa = 32: "sf"
aa = 2: staccato	aa = 35: "fz"
aa = 8: " > "	aa = 38: "sfz"
aa = 16: "^"	aa = 41: "rf"

Clefs

To define clefs, three parameters are available. They are clef type ("cl"), clef position on the staff ("li"), and octave transposition ("oc"). The method is suggested by the following examples:

cl = 0: C clef	li = 1: bottom line	oc = 0: no transposition
cl = 1: G clef	li = 3: middle line	oc = -1: one octave down
cl = 2: F clef	li = 5: top line	oc = +2: two octaves up

The treble clef would be cl = 1, li = 2, oc = 0. An *ottava bassa* transposition of the bass clef would be represented as cl = 2, li = 4, oc = -1, and so forth.

Other matters that are addressed in the proposed file extensions concern differentiation of part- ("track"-) specific information from global variables (for example, where time signatures may not be the same from part to part), graduated dynamics, and slurs.

SMDL: A Language for Music Documents

The American National Standards Institute committee on Musical Information Processing (MIPS), chaired by Charles Goldfarb, intends to issue a first draft of a proposed national Standard Music Description Language (SMDL) by the middle of 1991. The purpose of SMDL is to facilitate musical data interchange.

Over the past year the prospective standard has been divided into two projects. The time model that formed part of the original project, minus its provision for stress patterns, has been adopted as the basis for HyTime, a hyperdocument representation language with facilities for linking, anchoring, and synchronization. SMDL, which incorporates all other aspects of music description, has become one application of HyTime.

The MIPS secretariat is now located in Texas. The contact address is c/o Larry Austin, President, Computer Music Association, Box 1634, San Francisco, CA 94101-1634. Full texts of the draft standards for HyTime and SMDL can be requested as X3V1.8M/SD-7 and -8 respectively.

As a thesis project (M.S. in Computer Science), Neill Kipp at Florida State University has developed a program to convert SMDL documents to text file command sequences that can drive a synthesizer. The program consists of modules to facilitate lexical analysis, parsing, data structure managements, and output file generation. It is written in C.

To give some idea of what SMDL looks like, Neill Kipp and Steven R. Newcomb have provided a sample musical document description. Although only a two-bar sample is used, a general idea of the approach can be given. This representation is offered with several disclaimers. (1) Many options are available for SMDL representations. In the interest of brevity, neither the choices nor the reasons for making them are explained. (2) This example is relatively verbose because it is intended to be informative, but SMDL need not be so verbose. Standard Generalized Markup Language (SGML), a prototype document description language used for text representation, provides concise tags; a pre-parsed binary format is currently under development. (3) The line numbers do not form part of the document. (4) The indentation of elements is provided for clarity and has no other significance.

The symbolic grammar " < ... > " opens an element, while " < / ... > " closes it. "Gam" = *gamut*, the menu of available pitches. The *baton* is the beat. The *thread* is the musical voice.

Mary Had a Little Lamb

Ma - ry had a   lit - tle lamb

```
1    <work>
2
3    <bibdata>
4         <title>Mary Had a Little Lamb</title>
5    </bibdata>
6
7    <working class = excerpt>
8    <core>
9    <coredefs>
10   <pitchgam id = pitchgam>
11        gamutdes = "conventional 12-tone equal temperament"
12        highstep = 11
13        octratio = 2 1
14   >
15
16   <genfreq> -- sets gamstep 9 (= 'a') to be 440 Hz --
17        <gamstep>9</gamstep>
18        <freqspec> <hertz>440</hertz> </freqspec>
19   </genfreq>
20
21   <namestep>
22        <pitchdef> <pitchnm>c</pitchnm> <gamstep>0</gamstep> </pitchdef>
23   </namestep>
24   <namestep>
25        <pitchdef> <pitchnm>d</pitchnm> <gamstep>0</gamstep> </pitchdef>
26   </namestep>
27   <namestep>
28        <pitchdef> <pitchnm>e</pitchnm> <gamstep>0</gamstep> </pitchdef>
29   </namestep>
30   <namestep>
31        <pitchdef> <pitchnm>f</pitchnm> <gamstep>0</gamstep> </pitchdef>
32   </namestep>
33   <namestep>
34        <pitchdef> <pitchnm>g</pitchnm> <gamstep>0</gamstep> </pitchdef>
35   </namestep>
36   <namestep>
37        <pitchdef> <pitchnm>a</pitchnm> <gamstep>0</gamstep> </pitchdef>
38   </namestep>
39   <namestep>
40        <pitchdef> <pitchnm>b</pitchnm> <gamstep>0</gamstep> </pitchdef>
41   </namestep>
42   </pitchgam> </coredefs>
43   <baton id=baton1> <tempo> <musicdur> <vtu>4</vtu> </musicdur>
44   <realdur> <rtu rtubase = 1200>4800</rtu> </realdur> </tempo>
45   </baton>
46
```

```
47   <thread id = thread1
48       baton = baton1
49       nominst = voice>
50   <ces pitchgam = pitchgam0>
51   <ce --( Ma- )-->
52   <musicdur> <vtu> 1 2 </vtu> </musicdur>
53   <note> <nompitch> <gampitch> <octave> 2 </octave> <pitchnm>e</pitchnm>
54   </gampitch> </nompitch> </note>
55   </ce>
56   <ce --( ry- )-->
57   <musicdur> <vtu> 1 2 </vtu> </musicdur>
58   <note> <nompitch> <gampitch> <octave> 2 </octave> <pitchnm>e</pitchnm>
59   </gampitch> </nompitch> </note>
60   </ce>
61   <ce --( had- )-->
62   <musicdur> <vtu> 1 2 </vtu> </musicdur>
63   <note> <nompitch> <gampitch> <octave> 2 </octave> <pitchnm>e</pitchnm>
64   </gampitch> </nompitch> </note>
65   </ce>
66   <ce --( a )-->
67   <musicdur> <vtu> 1 2 </vtu> </musicdur>
68   <note> <nompitch> <gampitch> <octave> 2 </octave> <pitchnm>e</pitchnm>
69       </gampitch> </nompitch> </note>
70   </ce>
71   <ce --( lit- )-->
72   <musicdur> <vtu> 1 2 </vtu> </musicdur>
73   <note> <nompitch> <gampitch> <octave> 2 </octave> <pitchnm>e</pitchnm>
74   </gampitch> </nompitch> </note>
75   </ce>
76   <ce --( tle )-->
77   <musicdur> <vtu> 1 2 </vtu> </musicdur>
78   <note> <nompitch> <gampitch> <octave> 2 </octave> <pitchnm>e</pitchnm>
79   </gampitch> </nompitch> </note>
80   </ce>
81   <ce --( lamb )-->
82   <musicdur> <vtu> 1 2 </vtu> </musicdur>
83   <note> <nompitch> <gampitch> <octave> 2 </octave> <pitchnm>e</pitchnm>
84   </gampitch> </nompitch> </note>
85   </ce>
86   </ces>
87   </thread>
88   <lyric thread = thread1>
89   <syllable>Ma-</syllable>
90   <syllable>ry</syllable>
91   <syllable>had</syllable>
92   <syllable>a</syllable>
93   <syllable>lit-</syllable>
94   <syllable>tle</syllable>
95   <syllable>lamb</syllable>
96   </lyric>
97   </workseg>
98   </core>
99   </work>
```

The *Journal of Technical Development*, which is available from the MIPS secretariat [address given on p. 54], provides extensive explanations of the coding and its purposes.

TEI: The Text-Encoding Initiative

The Text-Encoding Initiative is intended to be to scholarly texts what SMDL is intended to be to music publications--a commonly accepted means of document markup that facilitates the interchange of texts in machine-readable form. The main objectives of the TEI are (1) to specify a common interchange format for text, (2) to provide guidelines for new text-encoding projects, (3) to document the major existing encoding schemes, and (4) to develop a metalanguage in which to describe them. Compatibility with existing standards, including Standard Generalized Markup Language (SGML), will be sought. The purpose of the interchange format is to specify how texts should be encoded so that they can be shared by different research projects and used for diverse purposes. The project is headed by C. M. Sperberg-McQueen. The first phase of the work, which has been funded by the National Endowment for the Humanities, the Commission of the European Communities, and the Andrew W. Mellon Foundation, culminated in a report that provided the basis for a one-day workshop at the ACH meeting in June 1990.

A provisional draft of the standard, *Guidelines for the Encoding and Interchange of Machine-Readable Texts* (1.0, August 1990) is available from Sperberg-McQueen at the Computer Center, M/C 135, University of Illinois at Chicago, Box 6998, Chicago, IL 60680, or from Lou Burnard, Oxford University Computing Service, 13 Banbury Road, Oxford OX2 6NN, England. Participation in an electronic discussion is possible through LISTSERV@UICVM. To join the group send the message SUBSCRIBE TEI-L <subscriber name>. TEI's draft may be of interest to musicologists who are extensively involved with print-oriented computer projects involving significant quantities of such literary documents as poems, dramas, scripts, or letters. Contributions may be sent to TEI-L@UICVM.

To give the flavor of the approach, we have constructed a bibliographical citation. It has two parts--the citation record as it would normally be given [<citn>] and a tagged set of fields [<citn.struct>]. In the first, the title is identified in order to facilitate typographical differentiation. A prospective publisher would, upon encountering this specification, insert an appropriate command to make the title appear in his or her house style (italics, small caps, etc.). The tagged fields in the second part of the record could facilitate interchange of information with a relational database or support free searches for designated kinds of information.

```
<list.citn>
        <citn>Winton Dean and John Merrill Knapp,
                <title>Handel's Operas, 1704-1726, </title>
                        (Oxford: Clarendon Press, 1987), 751 pp.
        </citn>

        <citn.struct>
                <authors>Winton Dean and John Merrill Knapp
                <title>Handel's Operas, 1704-1726
                <imprint>
                        <publ. city>Oxford
                        <publisher>Clarendon Press
                        <publ. date>1987
                </imprint>
                <detail>751 pp. </detail>
        </citn.struct>
</list.citn>
```

Bibliographical citations are discussed in Ch. 5 of the *Guidelines*.

SGML (ISO 8879) makes provision for treatment of diacriticals and some foreign alphabets. The topic of character representation is treated in Ch. 3. There are two lines of approach to the encoding of diacriticals. In one case, the diacritical is identified and a mark indicates the letter with which it is to be associated. In the other, a series of special alphabets storing particular letters with specific diacriticals is accessed. The first approach is adequate for modern European languages, where the alphabet is largely the same from language to language. The second is essential where the character set is distinctly different from country to country, as in ancient and oriental languages. One issue that has not been resolved by the group is whether to encourage a single approach to both sets of needs or to treat them differently.

CD+M

Warner New Media, which was instrumental in creating the CD+I (compact disk interactive) and CD+Graphics standards, is currently involved in negotiations with Philips and Sony to promote the development of specific standards for CD+M, compact disk plus MIDI technology. The basic idea is that MIDI data could be extracted from a performance recorded on CD. This extracted data could be exported to MIDI instruments and to music publishing programs. In contrast to CD+I technology, which depends on intensive indexing of the CD, and CD+Graphics, which deals with bit-mapped images, CD+M poses significant copyright problems [there is a brief discussion of these on p. 132].

Software

Software for Printing Music

Each spring CCARH sends out to the 75 or so developers of music printing software on its mailing list a packet of musical examples exhibiting problems which are special from a typographical point of view and essential capabilities from a musicological perspective. The developers have a window of approximately three months' time in which to respond. The solicitation is accompanied by a form requesting specific information about the hardware and software environment in which the program is run. This information is used in compiling the short descriptions that follow.

Developers often report in detail on those aspects of their products that are especially competitive. Heavily advertised products that are listed but not shown here are missing because no contribution was made. We have noted products that we learned of too late to contact. Some printing capabilities built into broad-spectrum MIDI programs are not oriented towards the needs of classical music.

Some developers respond every year; others prefer to respond only when new features have been added to their programs. Most software for printing classical music comes from small firms with few employees. Human problems such as illness, manpower shortages, equipment failure, and relocation sometimes undermine their efforts to respond punctually. Such difficulties prevented four potential contributors from meeting the deadline this year. We also report with regret the tragically premature death of Kimball Stickney, whose work on *High Score* was reported in previous issues, in May 1990.

Over the six years in which we have made this solicitation, the quality and availability of programs to print music have been enormously increased, but some of the issues in which users take the most interest remain incompletely addressed. Readers of *CM* are therefore encouraged to consult earlier issues to get a fuller picture of these issues. Since all developers are virtuosos at operating their own programs, the difficulty of duplicating the illustrations is a separate matter from assessing the quality of the output. Readers are urged to test programs personally before buying them. Prospective users may wish to consult these recent scholarly writings:

■ Garrett Bowles reviews "Music Notation Software for the IBM-PC" in *Notes* 46/3 (March 1990), 660-79. The programs included are *The Copyist III PC*, *DynaDuet*, *MusicPrinter Plus*, *The Note Processor*, *Personal Composer*, *SCORE*, and *Theme: The Music Editor*. The review is organized thematically. Attention extends to installation, documentation, online help, MIDI compatibility, symbol sets, screen editing, part extraction, transposition, page formatting, and special features. Communication concerning this review appears in *Notes* 47/1 (1990), 254-56.

■ Malcolm Butler and Nicholas Cook write on "Music Processing on the IBM: A Review of Available Systems" in *Current Musicology* No. 44 (1990), 61-98. Their article covers *The Note Processor*, the *Oberon Music Editor*, *Personal Composer*, *SCORE*, and *Theme: The Music Editor*. Each program was tested on an excerpt from Schumann's *Drei Romanzen*, Op. 94, and a Schenkerian graph and is considered separately. A generous number of examples is provided. There is a summary table of features. An update is planned.

■ Eric Graebner, Timothy Taylor, and Peter Allsop provide multiple user reports of *SCORE*, *HB Music Engraver*, and *Professional Composer* in *Musicus*, 1/1 (June 1989), pp. 39-87. Each author has different motivations for using such programs and reaches different conclusions.

■ Jon Grøver of the University of Oslo has recently completed a three-volume "Computer-Oriented Description of Music Notation." It is available at a modest cost from *Musikus*, Dept. of Music, University of Oslo, PO Box 1017, Blindern, N-0316 Oslo 2, Norway.

■ Keith A. Hamel describes "A Design for Music Editing and Printing Software based on Notational Syntax" in *Perspectives of New Music* 27/1 (1989), 70-83. Hamel is the developer of *NoteWriter*, but his article is a general one examining the strengths of a graphical approach to music representation for the purpose of printing.

Current and Recent Contributors

This listing concentrates on systems that have been represented by illustrations over the past three years and incorporates definitions of terms needed to understand the accounts given. Additional systems that are now dormant were cited in the *1987 Directory*, pp. 27-34. Music printing programs advertised in popular music magazines are listed here only if they have a demonstrated capability for handling classical music of moderate complexity.

A-R Music Engraver. A-R Editions, Inc., 801 Deming Way, Madison, WI 53717 (608-836-9000). A commercial version of the music typesetting system used by this publisher for its own editions and musical examples for academic journals has been developed for professional music publishing and is now available by license. Tom Hall is the principal developer. This version of the program, for the UNIX operating system, uses the NeWS and OpenWindows interfaces on the Sun SPARC workstation with a high resolution monitor (1600 x 1280). A version for the Sun-3 is also available. Music input is done alphanumerically with a modified version of DARMS; files may be created on networked PC-AT compatibles. Music can be edited on the screen. Scanned images from Macintosh PostScript programs can be imported.

A music notation library developed by A-R and multiple text fonts created by Mergenthaler are cross-licensed and available for use with the program. PostScript printers and typesetters are supported. The output shown is 1270 dpi from a Linotron L-300.

Alpha/TIMES. Kesselhaldenstr. 73, CH-9016 St. Gallen, Switzerland (41-71-35-1402). An integrated input and analysis system by Christoph Schnell for the Apple Macintosh line. TIMES stands for Totally Integrated Musicological Environment System. An unusual input method (voice recognition device with light pen) permits accurate reproduction of non-common notation, including neumes. The system incorporates graphics editors, a font editor, and a communication system. Illustrated in 1988 and previous years. No submission provided in 1989 or 1990.

Amadeus Music Software GmbH. Rohrauerstr. 50, Postfach 710267, D-8000 München 71, Germany (089-7855310). This product, originally developed by Kurt Maas, is commercially available for the PDP-11/73 and the Atari Mega ST4. Both alphanumeric and MIDI input are supported, the latter facilitating acoustical playback. Most data are stored as ASCII files. Screen editing is provided. Output (for dot matrix and laser printers, plotters, and phototypesetters) is scalable to a resolution of 1000 dots per inch.

Berlioz. Logiciel "Berlioz", Place des Lavoirs, F-30350 Lédignan, France (33-66-83-46-53). This is a series of three programs by Dominique Montel and Frédéric Magiera which are written in C for the Macintosh. The first program is for input, the second for layout, and the third for graphic editing. Input is created graphically. Extensive provisions for layout and graphic editing are provided. PostScript files for output to laser printers and phototypesetters are generated. *Berlioz*, which is in use at the printing establishment s.a.r.l. Dominique Montel, is also available for licensing.

CCARH. 525 Middlefield Rd., Ste. 120, Menlo Park, CA 94025 (415-322-7050). The Center's music representation system supports the development of electronic transcriptions and editions of a large quantity of musical repertory, chiefly from the eighteenth century. Input is from an electronic keyboard; alphanumeric code is used to provide non-acoustical information. A corollary music printing system, developed by Walter Hewlett, has been used to produce performing scores of several major works by Handel and Telemann. These capabilities are currently being implemented on a UNIX workstation. CCARH's input code was shown in the *1987 Directory*, p. 20.

Comus. Comus Music Printing and Publishing, Armthorpe, Tixall, Stafford ST18 0XP, England (0785-662520). The proprietary music printing program developed by John Dunn for this firm uses DARMS encoding of data with some newly devised extensions. The current version produces device-independent output in UNIX plot(5) format, which can be directed to screens, plotters, and laser printers.

The Copyist III. Dr. T's Music Software, 220 Boylston St., Suite 260, Chestnut Hill, MA 02167 (617-244-6954). Three versions of this commercial program for Atari, Amiga, and IBM PC compatibles are offered by Dr. T's. "III" is the most comprehensive version and the one best suited to academic applications. MIDI input and output are supported. Files can be converted to Tagged Image File Format (TIFF), a compressed representation of graphics information, and Encapsulated PostScript (EPS). Output supports PostScript and Ultrascript printers as well as the Hewlett Packard LaserJet Plus and plotters. *The Copyist* interfaces with a number of popular sequencer programs. The developer is Crispin Sion.

Dai Nippon Music Processor. Dai Nippon Printing Co., Ltd., CTS Division, 1-1 Ichigaya Kagacho 1-chome, Shinjuku-ku, Tokyo 162-01, Japan (Fax: 03-266-4199). This dedicated hardware system for the production of musical scores was announced three years ago and an illustration was last provided in 1988. Input is alphanumeric. Screen editing is supported. Output files can be sent to MIDI instruments, to PostScript printers, to a Digiset typesetter, or to the Standard Music Expression (SMX) file format used in music research at Waseda University. The Wagner example shown here was produced on a PostScript printer, while the German song ("O Tannenbaum") with Hiragana text underlay was produced on a Digiset typesetter. Kentaro Oka is the current manager.

Dal Molin Musicomp. 67 Florence Avenue, Oyster Bay, NY 11771 (516-922-7458). Armando Dal Molin has spent a lifetime in the effort to make music printing more efficient. More than 500,000 pages of music have been printed using equipment of his design. Examples were shown in 1988 and the internal code was indicated in the *1987 Directory*, p. 17. Dal Molin's Musicomp terminal is used by Belwin Mills Co.; a DOS version utilizing an auxiliary keypad for pitch entry is part of a larger package tailored to individual needs of existing users. The developer remains in contact with the Center and is eager to exchange ideas about computer music notation with other programmers but was unable to provide a contribution for this year.

Darbellay Music Processor. See **WOLFGANG**.

DARMS is an encoding system that originated in the 1960's. Various dialects have been used in several printing programs including those of A-R Editions, *The Note Processor*, and systems developed at the State University of New York at Binghamton by Harry Lincoln and at the University of Nottingham, England, by John Morehen. A sample of the code was shown in the *1987 Directory*, p. 12.

Deluxe Music Construction Set. Electronic Arts, 1820 Gateway Drive, San Mateo, CA 94404 (415-571-7171). This software program for the Macintosh line of computers produces PostScript files. Developed by Geoff Brown, it was last shown in 1987.

DynaDuet. DynaWare, 950 Tower Lane, #1150, Foster City, CA 94404 (415-349-5700). *DynaDuet*, a music printing program by Chris Geen for the IBM PC, accepts MIDI or alphanumeric input. The program's capabilities for classical music printing are under development. Output for 24-pin dot matrix printers is provided.

EASY KEY. John Clifton, 175 W. 87th St., Ste. 27E, New York, NY 10024 (212-724-1578). *Easy Key* simplifies the use of Jim Miller's *Personal Composer* input and printing program.

ERATO Music Manuscriptor. See under *Music Manuscriptor*.

ESCORT. Passport Designs, 625 Miramontes Street, Half Moon Bay, CA 94019 (415-726-0280). *Escort* facilitates input from a MIDI device to the *SCORE* printing program published by Passport.

EUTERPE. 99 rue Frédéric Mistral, F-03100 Montluçon, France (70-036903). *Euterpe* is a printing system under development by Michel Wallet. It forms part of an integrated system for encoding, printing, and analysis on the Macintosh. Special attention has been devoted to lute music and late Byzantine music. Transcription and conversion capabilities for German lute tablature to staff notation, based on programs by Bernard Stepien, were shown in 1988. The printing of Byzantine notation with text underlay in Cyrillic characters is shown in this issue.

FASTCODE. An encoding language of the 1970's developed at Princeton University for white mensural notation. An example of plotter output from 1981, first shown in 1985, is repeated in this issue.

Finale. Coda Music Software, Wenger Music Learning Systems, 1401 E. 79th St., Bloomington, MN 55420-1590 (612-854-1288). *Finale* has a broad range of capabilities related to music transcription and printing. MIDI files can be imported and exported. It provides immediate screen transcription of two-handed music. Four-part works played in two-stave arrangements may be "exploded" into four parts. Conversely, multi-voice music can be "imploded" to a piano reduction. Versions for the Apple Macintosh and the IBM PC are currently available; a version for the NeXT is under development. Data may also be entered alphanumerically. Finale's Enigma Transportable Files (ETF) are text files used to facilitate printing. *MusicProse* is a subset of *Finale* features made available at reduced cost and generally suited more to popular than to classical music.

Coda offers several music fonts—*Petrucci* for conventional notation, *Rameau* for subscripted chord names and basso continuo figures, *Seville* for guitar tablature, and *Newport* for jazz and percussion notation. *Finale* also provides support for mensural notation. PostScript printers are supported.

Phil Farrand developed the original program. Tim Herzog contributed illustrations in 1989 but has now left the firm, which failed to respond to enquiries in 1990.

Graphic Notes. See *Music Publisher*.

HB Music Engraver. HB Imaging, Inc., 560 South State Street, Orem, UT 84057 (801-225-7222). This printing program, distributed by HB Imaging, Inc., runs on the Apple Macintosh. Input is alphanumeric and utilizes redefinition of the QWERTY keyboard. HB output is for PostScript printers; a custom font called "Interlude" is available from the company. This program can convert files originated by another program, Mark of the Unicorn's *Professional Composer*. No contribution was received in 1989 or 1990.

HyperScribe. Coda Music Software, 1401 E. 79th St., Bloomington, MN 55420-1126 (612-854-1288). This product transcribes MIDI input to a Macintosh screen. It complements other products from Coda.

Interactive Music System (IMS). CERL Music Group, University of Illinois, 103 S. Mathews, #252, Urbana, IL 61801-2977 (217-333-0766). This extensive system has been under development at the University of Illinois since the early 1970's. It is based on the PLATO system, although extensions for the Macintosh and other microcomputers have been made in recent years. Music can be input from an alphanumeric code or from a synthesizer. The IMS was recently used to create a score and parts for the 1989 San Francisco Opera production of Vivaldi's *Orlando furioso* and to prepare a catalogue of music holdings of the Accademia Filarmonica in Bologna. Its printing capability was last shown in 1987, when its input and intermediate codes were given on pp. 18-9. A commercial version for the Macintosh is under development.

Laboratorio Informatica Musicale. Via Moretto da Brescia, 9, 20133 Milan, Italy. The LIM printing system, under development by Goffredo Haus, Luigi Finarelli and associates at the University of Milan, utilizes an Apple Macintosh. The system is designed to accept data in several codes and formats and forms part of a larger enterprise described on p. 127.

la mà de guido [Guido's Hand]. Apartat 23, E-08200, Sabadell (Barcelona), Spain (34-3-716-1350). This music printing software for IBM PC XT and AT computers uses an alphanumeric input system based on a redefined QWERTY keyboard (shown in the *1988 Directory*, p. 48). It is now being marketed as an input system for SCORE. MIDI playback and analysis are supported. Graphic output is by HPGL plotter or for PostScript printers of resolutions up to 2700 dpi. The developer is Llorenç Balsach.

Masterscore. Steinberg Jones, 17700 Raymer St., Ste. 1001, Northridge, CA 91325 (818-993-4091). This transcription program accepts MIDI input and outputs to various dot matrix printers by the firms Atari, Epson, NEC, and Star. It runs on an Atari ST. Shown in 1989.

MTeX is a set of fonts for music typesetting with the TeX document description language on mainframe computers. They were developed by Angelika Schofer and Andrea Steinbach at the Rheinische Friedrich-Wilhelms-Universität in Bonn. The set is available for DM 25 at Wegler Strasse 6, D-5300 Bonn, Germany.

MUSED. Oslo, Norway. This research system under development at Oslo University supports interactive analysis and music printing. Programs currently run on a VaxStation II. Examples of its representation and in-house printing system were shown in 1988. Commercial programs for music printing are also now in use.

Music Manuscriptor. Erato Software Corp., PO Box 6278, Salt Lake City, UT 84152-6278 (801-328-0500). This program operates as part of an integrated workstation for composition and orchestration. Setup requires an IBM PC compatible microcomputer, a digitizer tablet, and special graphics boards supporting a resolution of 800 x 1000 pixels. Pitches are entered as MIDI data; rhythmic assignment is automatic. Pattern storage (1000 slots) is provided for composition. Text underlay is available. Lines and pages can be justified automatically. A Breitkopf and Härtel font is available.

This product is compatible with two desktop publishing programs, *Ventura Publisher* and *Aldus Pagemaker*. Two laser printers, the Canon LBP8-11 and the Hewlett Packard LaserJet II, are supported. Erato takes pride in the compactness of its music files. The sizes of the complete files for the examples were as follows: Josquin—8 kilobytes, Bach Canon 1—3.4 kilobytes, Canon 2—3.2 kilobytes, and Wagner—8.7 kilobytes.

Music Publisher. Repertoire Pty. Ltd., 49A Stephens Terrace, St. Peters, 5069 Australia (618-363-2600). This program, developed by Trevor Richards for the Apple Macintosh, requires the use of a separate "presto pad" for input. Previously offered by Graphic Notes, it provides output for PostScript printers and typesetters. Examples were shown in 1988. No contribution was received in 1989 or 1990. The US distributor is InterSoft, 200 7th Ave., Suite 225, Santa Cruz, CA 95062 (408-476-1753).

MusicPrinter Plus. Temporal Acuity Products, Inc., 300 - 120th Avenue N.E., Bldg. 1, Bellevue, WA 98005 (800-426-2673). A manufacturer of interactive systems for rhythmic drill and other music teaching products, TAP's music printing program has evolved from one originally designed by Jack Jarrett for the Apple II to one for MS DOS machines. Version 3.0 permits MIDI entry of data; previous versions relied on graphic assembly of a score on the screen. The playback choices are quite sophisticated and extend to much subtlety of articulation. Playback can be in realtime or steptime, which can be forwards or backwards. Dot matrix, laser, and ink jet printers are supported. Wide-carriage output on the BJ-130 provides 360 dpi resolution.

MusicProse. See *Finale*.

Musicwriter II. See **The Portable Musicwriter**.

MusiKrafters. MusiKrafters, PO Box 14124, Louisville, KY 40214 (502-361-4597). This software company offers special-purpose products by Robert Fruehwald for musical excerpts and unusual notations for the Apple Macintosh. Input is alphanumeric and may be edited on the screen. PostScript files are produced. Its shape-note and tablature capabilities were shown in 1988 and a HyperText program for musical information management was shown in 1989. No contribution was received in 1990.

MusScribe. See *NoteWriter*.

MUSTRAN. This alphanumeric code was developed at Indiana University by Jerome Wenker in the 1960's. Music printing capabilities were extended by Don Byrd; music encoded in MUSTRAN has been used for analytical programs by Dorothy Gross, Gary Wittlich, and others.

Nightingale. Opcode Systems, 3641 Haven Avenue, Menlo Park, CA 94025 (415-321-8977). Don Byrd's program for music notation, shown in previous years, runs on the Apple Macintosh and is soon to be released. *Nightingale* uses MIDI input. Byrd is in residence at the Center for Research on Concepts and Cognition, headed by Douglas Hofstadter, at Indiana University in 1990-91. Output has been shown in four previous issues.

The Note Processor. Thoughtprocessors, 584 Bergen Street, Brooklyn, NY 11238 (718-857-2860). Stephen Dydo's program for IBM PC compatibles accepts both alphanumeric and MIDI input; data can be edited either through code revisions or by using a mouse. The input is a slightly modified version of DARMS; an example of *NP*'s representation scheme was shown in the *1987 Directory*, p. 13. Numerous dot matrix printers as well as the Hewlett Packard DeskJet and LaserJet printers are supported. Optically scanned data from the Ottawa group [see p. 42] is printed via this program.

NoteWriter. Passport Designs, 625 Miramontes, Half Moon Bay, CA 94019 (415-726-0280). This commercial product for the Apple Macintosh is the heir of *MusScribe* (shown in 1988) and has been developed by Keith Hamel of Richmond, BC. *NoteWriter* is used to typeset the musical examples in *Perspectives of New Music* and in the popular music publications of the GPI Corp. in Cupertino, CA. Hamel describes his approach to music printing in the Winter 1989 issue of *Perspectives*.

Oberon Music Editor. Oberon Systems, PO Box 4179, Boulder, CO 80306-4179 (303-459-3411). This program for IBM PC compatibles is available as a stand-alone product or on a license basis. Entry is alphanumeric and supports printing only. A custom font, Callisto, and a multi-size font set called Publisher Series are available. A shape-note version of the Editor is also available. Output devices supported include the Hewlett Packard LaserJet and DeskJet series as well as various 9- and 24-pin dot matrix printers. Musical examples can be integrated with *WordPerfect* files and output to PostScript printers. Compatibility with *Ventura Publisher* is currently being implemented. Although Oberon is intended primarily for transcription and printing, those wishing to build data analysis tools around the Oberon music file format can receive assistance from Joel Grossman at the above address.

PARD. PARD S.r.L., Via Cavalcante, 8, I-20127 Milan, Italy. This music printing system, under development in 1988 by Walter Prati and Giorgio Ceroni, was mainframe based, with plotter output. Examples of its work were shown in 1988.

Personal Composer. Jim Miller, PO Box 648, Honaunau, HI 96726 (808-328-9518). This program by Jim Miller for the IBM PC line accepts MIDI input and outputs Postscript files. See the *1987 Directory*. No contribution was received in 1988, 1989, or 1990. See also *Easy Key*.

Philip's Music Scribe (PMS). 33 Metcalfe Road, Cambridge CB4 2DB, England (44-223-65518). This program by Philip Hazel for the Acorn Archimedes workstation uses alphanumeric input and produces PostScript files for output. Acorn products are currently available in the UK and Europe. *PMS*, which is available by license only, has extensive capabilities for accommodating the needs of parts and scores derived from a common file. Staves can be overlaid, permitting four-part choral music to be shown on two staves, for example. Up to four verses of text underlay can be accommodated. Slur control is extensive. Basso continuo figuration is supported. Time signatures can be switched off. All characters found in the *PMS* music font set are also available for use in text strings. The output shown is from an Apple LaserWriter (300 dpi).

Plaine and Easie. This melodic input code developed by Barry Brook and Murray Gould in the late 1960's remains important because of its extensive use in thematic indexing projects, especially the manuscript cataloguing effort of the International Inventory of Musical Sources (RISM) coordinated in Frankfurt, Germany. Diverse printing programs for RISM data have been written. Output from one by Norbert Böker-Heil was shown in the *1986 Directory*, p. 19. A program for conversion of *Plaine and Easie* code to CCARH files has recently been written by Brent Field. Documentation of the code is available from RISM Zentralredaktion, Sopienstr. 26, D-6000 Frankfurt-am-Main 90, Germany.

PLAINSONG. Surrey, England. PLAINSONG is a series of programs for transcription, analysis, and printing of music in black square neumatic notation on a four-line stave with C, F, D, or G clefs. It is under development by Catherine Harbor and Andy Reid at Royal Holloway and Bedford New College (Computer Centre, Egham Hill, Egham, Surrey, UK TW20 0EX; C. Harbor@vax.rhbnc.ac.uk). PLAINSONG runs on the IBM PC. Dot matrix and PostScript laser printers may be used.

The Portable Musicwriter. Music Print Corp., 2620 Lafayette Drive, Boulder, CO 80303. This method for printing musical examples, developed by Cecil Effinger, a recognized pioneer in music printing technology, requires an IBM Wheelwriter. The resolution is 104 dpi vertically and 120 dpi horizontally. Music is represented alphanumerically. Slurs are added by hand.

Professional Composer. Mark of the Unicorn, 222 Third St., Cambridge, MA 02142 (617-576-2760). This commercial product for the Apple Macintosh has been poorly represented in previous years because of its failure to provide any material other than advertising copy. Its one contribution was shown in 1988.

SCORE. Passport Designs, 625 Miramontes Street, Half Moon Bay, CA 94019 (415-726-0280). Deriving from an academic research system at Stanford University, Leland Smith's SCORE program for IBM PC compatibles is now in use by major music publishers such as Schott and several performing organizations. SCORE is also being used to produce the collected works of J.-B. Lully. Optically scanned musical data from the University of Surrey have been converted to SCORE data for printing. The input is alphanumeric and requires separate passes for pitch, rhythm, and articulation. Forty music fonts are available. There is a PostScript text font compatibility. The SCORE input code was shown in the *1987 Directory*, p. 14. See also *Escort, la mà de guido,* and *ScoreInput.*

ScoreInput. Modular Music, 6800 Red Top Road #1, Takoma Park, MD 20912-5920 (301-270-1095). ScoreInput is a program by Paul Nahay to generate input for Leland Smith's SCORE program either from a MIDI keyboard or through redefinition of a QWERTY keyboard. The developer claims that it is faster and more accurate than other front ends for SCORE. ScoreInput writes one ASCII file that instructs SCORE to assemble the score and save each system to its own graphics file.

ScoreWriter. Sonus Corp., 21430 Strathern St., Ste. H, Canoga Park, CA 91304 (818-702-0992). This is a MIDI input transcription program for the Atari. No information on output devices was provided. Shown in 1989.

SCRIBE. Scribe Software Associates, La Trobe University, Bundoora, Victoria 3083, Australia (03-479-2879). The academic research system developed jointly by La Trobe and Melbourne Universities for fourteenth-century music is oriented mainly toward database management of musical repertories. It runs on IBM PC AT-compatibles. It handles entry, display, retrieval, and analysis. Its capability for producing facsimiles of sources with any Hewlett Packard compatible plotter extends to colored notation. A plotter driver for round notation is under development. Single attributes (e.g., pitch) may be searched. User-entered data can be merged with pre-packaged data for analytical use. The program is available by license to both individuals and institutional sites and runs in IBM PC compatibles. The original software development was by John Griffiths; John Stinson is the head musicologist. The current software developer is Brian Parish. User support is available by fax (03-478-5814) and electronic mail (musjs@latvax8.lat.oz).

Staatliches Institut für Musikforschung. Tiergarten Str. 1, D-1000 Berlin 30, Germany. Music printing programs written in FORTRAN in the early 1970's by Norbert Böker-Heil for IBM 360 input and output from a Digiset T 41 typesetter are currently under revision. The new programs will be written in C, will operate initially under MS DOS and later under the UNIX operating system, and will be PostScript compatible. The existing system has been used to produce scores for music publishers. Questions regarding its use may be directed to the firm of Satz-Rechen-Zentrum in Berlin. Some special capabilities of the system for contemporary music were shown in the *1988 Directory,* pp.122-5.

Renaissance mensural notation that runs on a Macintosh Plus with HyperCard. Transcriptions are assembled on the screen from graphic elements. The price is extremely modest. Examples including "illuminated" initials, ligatures, and white mensural notation were shown in 1989.

Synclavier Music Engraving System. PO Box 546, 49 N. Main St., White River Junction, VT 05001 (802-295-5800). The Music Engraving System offered by New England Digital Corp. is designed exclusively for use with its Synclavier digital audio system. Information can be entered alphanumerically, via MIDI input, or by on-screen assembly. Some special capabilities, including shape notes and tablatures, are available. PostScript files are produced. Gregg Sewell, an engraver at 518 N. Cherry St., Florence, AL 35630 (205-764-6212), has provided examples for recent issues of this publication.

TELETAU. Pisa and Florence, Italy. *TELETAU* is an integrated system for musical data management initially developed at CNUCE in Pisa; it is now maintained jointly with the Florence Conservatory. It has a library of 800 encoded works and numerous analysis programs. Details of its encoding system were shown in the *1987 Directory*, p. 22. See the index for other information related to this system.

THEME, The Music Editor. PO Box 8204, Charlottesville, VA 22906 (804-971-5963). This commercial product, developed by Mark Lambert for the IBM PC, has been used extensively in academic settings. Its alphanumeric input system uses a redefined keyboard (shown in 1988). It has a provision for MIDI input and for conversion of alphanumeric files to MIDI output. Optimization of page layout is automatic. Binary-encoded data sets are available to users. *THEME* has recently moved to new premises.

TIFF. The Tagged Image File Format (TIFF) facilitates interchange of graphics files between programs. Musical notation created with a printing program that provides this option can be exported to a word processor program, for example. Other graphics file conversion formats include *DXF*, which supports AutoCAD, *EPS*, Encapsulated PostScript, which creates files for a PostScript printer, and *HPGL*, a Hewlett-Packard Graphics Language Plotter File.

Toppan Scan-Note System. Toppan International Group, Iwanami Shoten Annex Bldg. 2-3-1, Kanda Jimbocho, Chiyoda-ku, Tokyo 101, Japan. The Toppan system originated in Aarhus, Denmark, where it was developed by Mogens Kjaer. It is at present a proprietary system that accepts electronic keyboard input and prints music with a laser phototypesetter. Toppan Printing Co. Ltd. contracts with major music publishers and has produced some recent volumes of the *Neue Mozart Ausgabe*. Illustrations were shown in 1987.

produced some recent volumes of the *Neue Mozart Ausgabe*. Illustrations were shown in 1987.

WOLFGANG. Société Mus'Art, Case Postale 26, CH-1242 Satigny, Geneva, Switzerland. This academically oriented music processor, developed by Etienne Darbellay for IBM PC compatibles, became commercially available within the past year and was awarded the Swiss Prize for Technology for 1990.

It was illustrated in 1988 and previous years. The keyboard is fully user definable. Screen resolutions to 1664 x 1200 are supported. Files can be converted to TIFF compressed or uncompressed formats and used with such desktop publishing programs as *Ventura Publisher* and *Aldus Pagemaker*. Dot matrix and LaserJet output is supported. PostScript support is under development, as is an interface for MIDI input. An interface with the ADLIB sound driver exists.

WOLFGANG has the ability to represent and reproduce plain chant, mensural notation (black and white, ligatures), and the unmeasured *style brisé*. It also supports automatic reduction to a two-stave transcription of up to five voices and permits the creation of polylingual scores requiring Arabic, Cyrillic, and Gothic (as well as Roman) characters.

Comments on the Illustrations

Edmund Correia, Jr.

Each year's examples have introduced new problems. This year the set pieces were short quotations from (1) Bach's *Musical Offering*, (2) the *Agnus Dei* III from Josquin's *Mass of the Blessed Virgin*, and (3) Act One of Wagner's *Götterdämmerung*.

The canons from *The Musical Offering* present several cases of non-standard placement of clefs and signatures. It was not noticed until studying the responses of our contributors that our source for this example, the *Bach Gesellschaft* edition, contains a small error. The second of the two canons used ends with a time signature which was inverted rather than reversed left-to-right (as were the key signature and clef). Although some contributors discovered and corrected this error, it should be assumed that the others were faithfully reproducing the example as requested.

More significant differences may be discovered in the settings of the lengthier Josquin and Wagner pieces. It was permissible here to shorten the excerpts somewhat, if that would allow for a more readable, less congested appearance. The main problem in the Josquin is the placement of bar lines between the staves, a practice often found in scholarly editions of Renaissance music to reduce accentual emphasis based on barring. Those who could not support this feature were asked simply to use conventional bar lines.

Spacing between staves and systems, and between vocal lines and corresponding text also contributes to the differences in clarity and overall appearance.

We were pleasantly surprised that so many contributors were willing to confront the daunting tangle of slurs, ties, tuplets, tremolos, arpeggiation, dynamics, accidentals, and other details encountered in the Wagner piano transcription. The results are good to excellent, yet (understandably) only one setting is completely free of errors or omissions. Fingering numbers offer an interesting point of comparison: size, font style, and placement vary widely, and some solutions are probably an improvement over our source edition.

Among the free choices, #27 displays text underlay in Hiragana [the name of the translator is in Kanji in the upper left], #28 includes elements of colored notation in the music of Frescobaldi, #29 uses all seven shapes of the shape-note system developed to facilitate the learning of sacred music in the rural American South and Midwest, #30 shows an automatic transcription into conventional notation of German lute tablature, and #31 demonstrates a capability for simultaneous handling of texts in Greek and Old Church Slavonic.

List of Illustrations

The illustrations are arranged alphabetically first by the surname of the composer and second by the surname of the contributor. Illustrations are unretouched. Printer designations identify the specific configuration used to produce the example. The originating hardware is indicate in this listing.

Bach: *The Musical Offering*

1. IBM PC		*Oberon Music Editor*
2. IBM PC		*Wolfgang*
3. IBM Wheelwriter		*The Portable Musicwriter*
4. PDP-11/73; Atari ST4		*Amadeus Music Software*
5. Erato workstation		*Erato Music Manuscriptor*
6. IBM PC		*SCORE*

Josquin: *Agnus Dei* from the *Mass of the Blessed Virgin*

7. IBM PC	*la mà de guido*
8. IBM PC	*Oberon Music Editor*
9. Archimedes workstation	*Philip's Music Scribe*
10. PDP-11/73; Atari ST4	*Amadeus Music Software*
11. Macintosh	*Berlioz*
12. Erato workstation	*Erato Music Manuscriptor*
13. IBM PC	*SCORE*
14. Sun workstation (Sun-3 or SPARC)	*A-R Music Engraving System*
15. IBM PC	*The Note Processor*

Wagner: from Act One of *Götterdämmerung*

16. Dai Nippon Music Processor	*Dai Nippon Music Processor*
17. IBM PC	*Wolfgang*
18. IBM Wheelwriter	*The Portable Musicwriter*
19. Archimedes workstation	*Philip's Music Scribe*
20. PDP-11/73; Atari	*Amadeus Music Software*
21. Macintosh	*Berlioz*
22. Atari ST	*The Copyist III*
23. IBM PC	*SCORE*
24. Synclavier	*Synclavier Music Engraving System*
25. Sun workstation (Sun-3 or SPARC)	*A-R Music Engraving System*
26. IBM PC	*The Note Processor*

Free choices:

27. *Dai Nippon Music Processor*—folk song with Hiragana text underlay
28. *Wolfgang*—colored notation from the seventeenth century [Frescobaldi]
29. *Synclavier Music Engraving System*—hymn with shape notes
30. *Euterpe*—automatic transcription of lute tablature
31. *A-R Music Engraving System*—chant with Greek and Slavonic text underlay

Illustration 1

Contributor: Nancy Colton
Product: Oberon Music Editor
Running on: IBM PC compatibles

Output from: Hewlett Packard DeskJet
Size as shown: 100% of original

Canon perpetuus
super thema regium

Canones diversi
super thema regium

Canon a 2.

Illustration 2

Contributor: Etienne Darbellay
Product: WOLFGANG by Mus'Art
Running on: IBM PC compatibles

Output from: HP LaserJet III
Size as shown: 100% of original

Canon perpetuus
super thema regium.

Canones diversi
super thema regium.

Illustration 3

Contributor: Cecil Effinger
Product: The Portable Musicwriter
Input device: The Portable Musicwriter

Output device: IBM Wheelwriter
Size as shown: 60% of original

Canon perpetuus
super thema reglum

Canones diversi
super thema reglum

Canon a 2.

1.

Illustration 4

Contributor: Kurt Maas   **Output device:** Amadeus ECRM Lasersetter (1000 dpi)
Product: Amadeus Music Software   **Size as shown:** 100% of original
Running on : a PDP-11/73; Atari Mega ST4

Canon perpetuus
super thema regium.

Canones diversi
super thema regium.

amadeus *music software*

Illustration 5

Contributor: Jeffrey L. Price
Product: Erato Music Manuscriptor
Running on: Erato workstation

Output from: Hewlett Packard LaserJet II
Size as shown: 74% of original

Illustration 6

Contributor: Leland Smith
Product: SCORE from Passport Designs
Running on: IBM PC compatibles

Output device: Verityper (1250 dpi)
Size as shown: 92% of original

Canon perpetuus
super thema regium

Canones diversi
super thema regium

Canones diversi
super thema regium
(performance score)

Illustration 7

Contributor: Llorenç Balsach
Product: la mà de guido
Running on: IBM PC/AT compatibles

Output device: QMS
Size as shown: 100% of original

Illustration 8

Contributor: Nancy Colton
Product: Oberon Music Editor
Running on: IBM PC compatibles

Output from: Hewlett Packard DeskJet
Size as shown: 100% of original

Illustration 9

Contributor: Philip Hazel   **Output device:** Apple Laserwriter
Product: Philip's Music Scribe   **Size as shown:** 100% of original
Running on : Acorn Archimedes workstation

Missa de Beato Vergine, Agnus Dei

Josquin

Illustration 10

Contributor: Kurt Maas
Product: Amadeus Music Software
Running on : a PDP-11/73; Atari Mega ST4

Output device: Amadeus ECRM Lasersetter (1000 dpi)
Size as shown: 100% of original

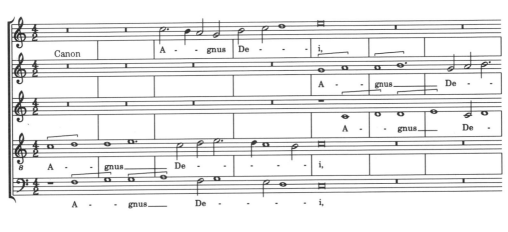

Illustration 11

Contributors: Dominique Montel, Frédéric Magiera
Product: Berlioz
Running on: Apple Macintosh

Output device: Linotronic 300
Size as shown: 100% of original

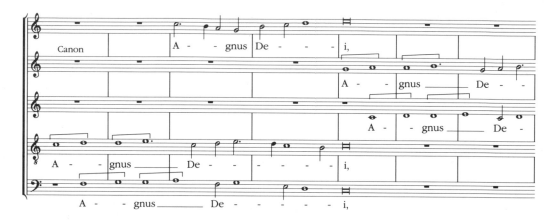

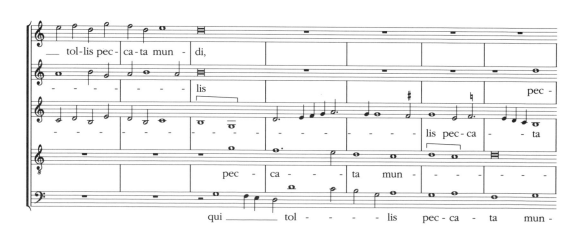

Illustration 12

Contributor: Jeffrey L. Price
Product: Erato Music Manuscriptor
Running on: Erato workstation

Output from: Hewlett Packard LaserJet II
Size as shown: 73% of original

Josquin Desprez
Missa de Beato Vergine
Agnus Dei

Illustration 13

Contributor: Leland Smith
Product: SCORE from Passport Designs
Running on: IBM PC compatibles

Output device: Verityper (1250 dpi)
Size as shown: 92% of original

Illustration 14

Contributor: Rolf Wulfsberg
Product: A-R Music Engraving System
Running on: Sun-3 or SPARC station

Output device: Linotype L-300 (1270 dpi)
Size as shown: 100% of original

Illustration 15

Contributor: Stephen Dydo
Product: Thoughtprocessors' Note Processor
Running on: IBM PC compatibles

Output from: Hewlett Packard DeskJet
Size as shown: 100% of original

Illustration 16

Contributor: Dai Nippon Printing Co., Ltd.

Output device: Hell's Digiset

Product: Dai Nippon Music Processor

Size as shown: 78% of original

Input device: Dai Nippon Music Processor

Illustration 17

Contributor: Etienne Darbellay
Product: WOLFGANG by Mus'Art
Running on: IBM PC compatibles

Output from: HP LaserJet III
Size as shown: 100% of original

Illustration 18

Contributor: Cecil Effinger
Product: The Portable Musicwriter
Input device: The Portable Musicwriter

Output device: IBM Wheelwriter
Size as shown: 60% of original

Illustration 19

Contributor: Philip Hazel   **Output device:** Apple Laserwriter
Product: Philip's Music Scribe   **Size as shown:** 78% of original
Running on: Acorn Archimedes workstation

Götterdammerung, Act I

Illustration 20

Contributor: Kurt Maas
Product: Amadeus Music Software
Running on: a PDP-11/73; Atari Mega ST4

Output device: Amadeus ECRM Lasersetter (1000 dpi)
Size as shown: 100% of original

Illustration 21

Contributors: Dominique Montel, Frédéric Magiera
Product: Berlioz
Running on: Apple Macintosh

Output device: Linotronic 300
Size as shown: 75% of original

Illustration 22

Contributor: Crispin Sion
Product: The Copyist [from Dr. T's Music Software]
Running on: Atari ST

Output device: QMS PS 800+
Size as shown: 78% of original

Illustration 23

Contributor: Leland Smith   **Output device:** Verityper (1250 dpi)
Product: SCORE from Passport Designs   **Size as shown:** 92% of original
Running on: IBM PC compatibles

#3. Wagner
Götterdammerung, Act I

Illustration 24

Contributor: Alan Talbot
Product: Synclavier Music Engraving System
Input device: Synclavier Digital Audio System

Output device: Linotronic 100 Imagesetter (1270 dpi)
Size as shown: 100% of original
Engraver: Gregg Sewell

Illustration 25

Contributor: Rolf Wulfsberg
Product: A-R Music Engraving System
Running on: Sun-3 or SPARC station

Output device: Linotype L-300 (1270 dpi)
Size as shown: 100% of original

Illustration 26

Contributor: Stephen Dydo
Product: Thoughtprocessors' Note Processor
Running on: IBM PC compatibles

Output from: Hewlett Packard DeskJet
Size as shown: 100% of original

Illustration 27

Contributor: Dai Nippon Printing Co., Ltd.
Product: Dai Nippon Music Processor
Input device: Dai Nippon Music Processor

Output device: Sony LBP, NWP-533
Size as shown: 78% of original

桃 園 京 子 　訳詞

Volksweise

1. も　　み　の　き　も　み　の　き　こ　か　げ　は　か　な　し
2. お　　と　め　よ　お　と　め　よ　お　も　か　げ　い　ず　こ

さ　さ　や　き　あ　ゆ　み　し　お　も　い　で　ひ　そ　め　て　も
や　さ　し　き　ち　か　い　を　こ　か　げ　に　の　こ　し　て　お

み　の　き　も　み　の　き　か　え　ら　ぬ　あ　の　ひ
と　め　よ　お　と　め　よ　か　な　し　き　ゆ　め　よ

Illustration 28

Contributor: Etienne Darbellay
Product: WOLFGANG by Mus'Art
Running on: IBM PC compatibles

Output from: HP LaserJet III
Size as shown: 70% of original

ARIA DETTA BALLETTO

G. Frescobaldi
Secondo Libro di Toccate

The filled whole notes and void eight notes shown here constitute "colored" notation expressing accents that contradict the assigned meter [see p. 26].

Illustration 29

Contributor: Alan Talbot   **Output device:** Linotronic 100 Imagesetter (1270 dpi)
Product: Synclavier Music Engraving System   **Size as shown:** 100% of original
Input device: Synclavier Digital Audio System   **Engraver:** Gregg Sewell

On Jordan's Bank the Baptist's Cry

1. On Jor - dan's bank the Bap - tist's cry An -
2. Then cleansed be ev - 'ry breast from sin; Make
3. For thou art our sal - va - tion, Lord, Our
4. To heal the sick stretch out thy hand, And

noun - ces that the Lord is nigh; A - wake, and hark - en,
straight the way for God with - in, And let each heart pre -
ref - uge, and our great re - ward; With - out thy grace we
bid the fall - en sin - ner stand; Shine forth, and let thy

for he brings Glad tid - ings of the King of kings.
pare a home Where such a might - y guest may come.
waste a - way Like flow'rs that with - er and de - cay.
light re - store Earth's own true lov - li - ness once more.

5. All praise, eternal Son, to thee,
   Whose advent doth thy people free;
   Whom with the Father we adore
   And Holy Spirit evermore.

Illustration 30

Contributor: Michel Wallet
Product: Euterpe (for ERATTO interface)
Running on: Apple Macintosh

Output device: Hewlett Packard LaserJet
Size as shown: 67% of original

Illustration 31

Contributor: Rolf Wulfsberg
Product: A-R Music Engraving System
Running on: Sun-3 or SPARC station

Output device: Linotype L-300 (1270 dpi)
Size as shown: 78% of original

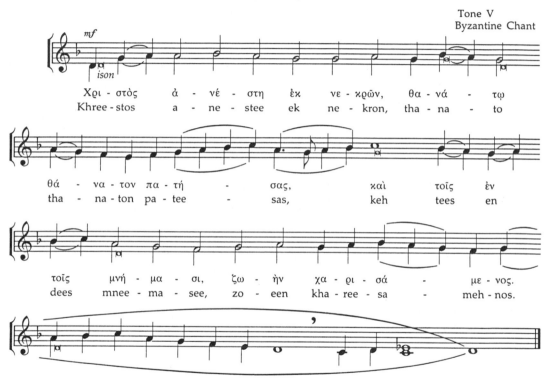

Paschal Troparion
(In Greek)

Tone V
Byzantine Chant

Paschal Troparion
(In Church Slavonic)

Tone V
Znamennyj Chant

Dance Notation Software

The Hungarian dancer Rudolf von Laban developed a now widely used system of movement notation in the early part of this century. Labanotation is read from bottom to top. It may be laid out in multiple columns and these may be interleaved with conventional staff notation that is rotated 90 degrees counterclockwise.

Labanotation comprises two kinds of symbols—those of constant size (pins, pre-signs, and space measurement signs) and those of variable length (directions, rotations, and pathways). Early efforts to computerize the drawing of Labanotation were made at the Moore School of Electrical Engineering in Philadelphia, at the University of Iowa, and by Elsie Dunin (*LC's LN*) at the University of California at Los Angeles. Two fully functional programs to print Labanotation, *Calaban* and *LabanWriter*, are described and illustrated on the following pages.

Programs for dance notation not based on Laban's system include two developed in Canada—the University of Waterloo's *MacBenesh*, using the left-to-right Benesh system, and Simon Fraser University's *Compose*, which uses stick figures—and one in England, *Kinotate*, a program for the BBC microcomputer developed at the Birmingham Polytechnic.

Calaban

Calaban, developed by Andy Adamson at the University of Birmingham (England), is a Labanotation implementation of computer-aided design. It is intended for professional choreographers and dance researchers. It runs on both IBM equipment with AutoCAD and on the Macintosh IIx. Information is entered into the computer with a digitizing tablet. This tablet is overlaid with a grid showing the location of the notation symbols, which are selected from a library of dance symbols in common usage. A personal library of frequently used movements may be defined to facilitate both the creation of scores and the structural analysis of stored works.

Final copy may be produced by a graphics plotter, a laser printer, or a phototypesetter. Commercial desktop publishing programs enable notation created with AutoCad to be integrated into larger documents. Scores of as many as 100 pages have been created using *Calaban*. Information on *Calaban* can be obtained from Andy Adamson, Department of Drama and Theatre Arts, The University of Birmingham, PO Box 363, Birmingham B15 2TT, UK (021-414-6005).

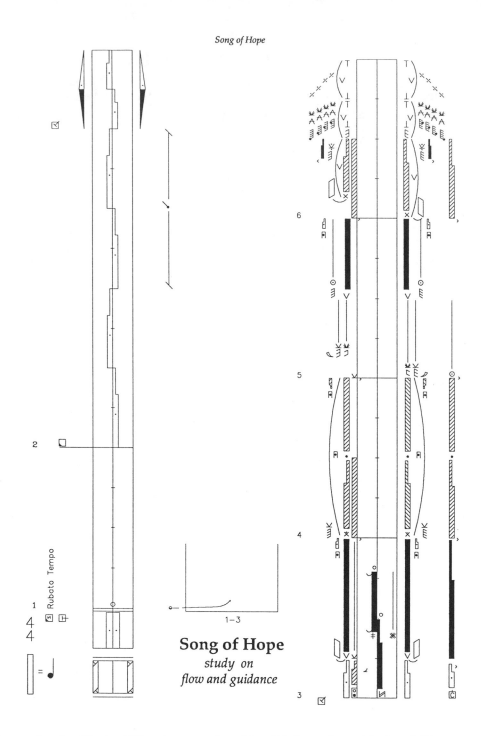

Song of Hope

Song of Hope
study on
flow and guidance

Labanotation for "Song of Hope" was produced by *Calaban* using a Macintosh IIx computer. The output from an Apple LaserWriter IINT.

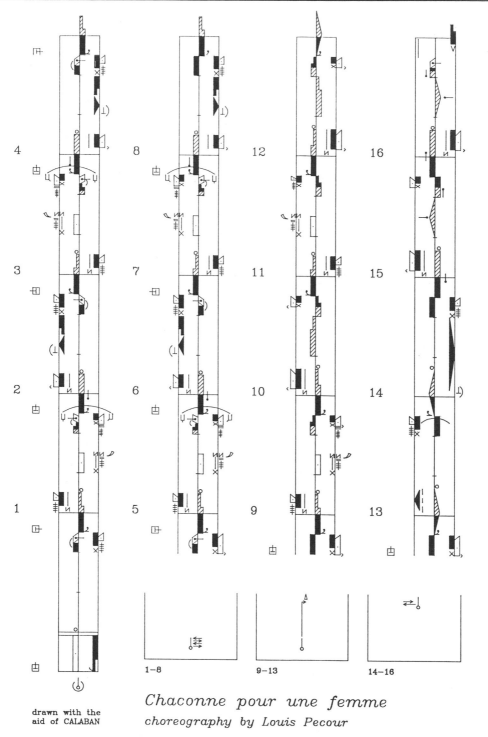

Chaconne pour une femme

choreography by Louis Pecour

drawn with the
aid of CALABAN

Labanotation for "Chaconne pour une femme" was created by *Calaban* using an IBM PC AT. The output is from liquid ink pens in a flatbed plotter.

LabanWriter

LabanWriter, which is described as a word processor for Labanotation, has been developed at the Ohio State University by George Karl and Scott Sutherland. Their work has been sponsored by the Dance Notation Bureau Extension, directed by Lucy Venable. The program runs on Apple Macintosh computers. More than 600 symbols provide references to moving parts of the body, types of movements, their directions, and durations. Users can also add symbols of their own. *LabanWriter* documents can be exported to painting, drawing and word processor files for further modification. The project, which was initiated in 1984, has received support from The Ohio State University, from the Department of Dance, and from the Andrew W. Mellon Foundation. The first score was produced in the spring of 1989.

The program has also been used in an anthropology project at Indiana University to record the sign language of the Plains Indians. If it follows in the path of manually drawn Labanotation, it may be used for notating gymnastics events, time-and-motion studies, animal behavior, physical therapy exercises, computer animation, and designs for robotics control.

LabanWriter is available without charge, with the provision that any copies made by users include both the manual and the software. For a small subscription fee, updates will be sent as they become available. For further information contact *LabanWriter*, Department of Dance, 1813 N. High St., Columbus, OH 43210.

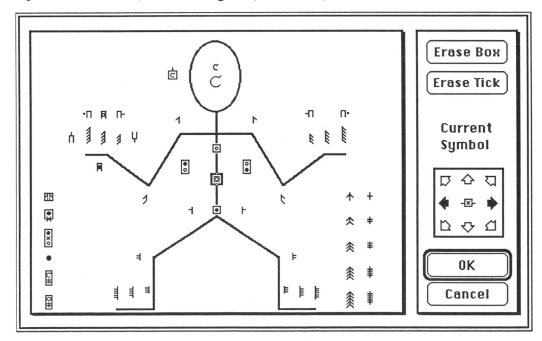

Screen configuration of the figure palette, one of twelve menus available with *LabanWriter*.

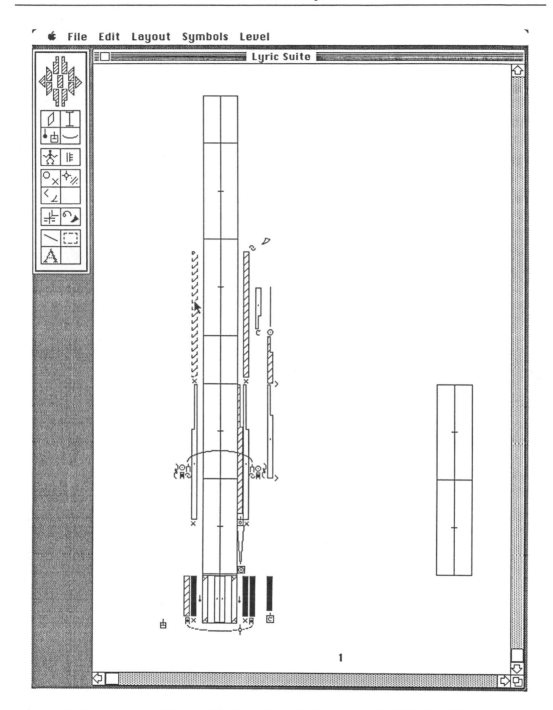

A few measures of Anna Sokolow's *Lyric Suite* produced with *LabanWriter*.

A directional symbol is being placed by the cursor on the staff. The main palette in the upper left corner includes the main directional symbols plus eleven buttons which bring up the other palettes as well as a line drawing tool, a text tool, and a selection box.

Software for Theory and Analysis

Classroom Software—Music Theory

Counterpoint

Palestrina introduces students to two-part counterpoint in first, second, and fourth species. It runs on the Macintosh. The program identifies modes, detects errors, and stores rules. Screen size limits the length of examples, and the choice of only whole and half notes limits the complexity of what can be created. *Palestrina* was developed at Dartmouth College (Hanover, NH 03755) by David E. Jones and John R. Meier and is distributed in the US by Kinko's.

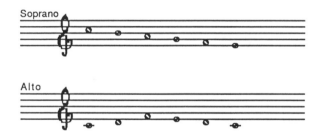

Two-part counterpoint in first species created with *Palestrina*.

Ear Training

Practica Musica is an interactive drill-and-review ear-training and music-theory program for the Macintosh. Dictation exercises use selections from the entire history of music (in contrast to the computer-generated melodies used by some other ear-training programs). New material can be created by the user from a MIDI keyboard or an onscreen picture of a keyboard. *Practica Musica* is a commercial program from Ars Nova Software, PO Box 637, Kirkland, WA 98083; telephone (800) 445-4866.

Harmony

Harmony Coach by John William Schaffer (School of Music, 455 N. Park St., University of Wisconsin, Madison, WI 53706) allows students to classify harmonies into general chord classes and to structure "lower levels of information specific to distinctive chord groups." It is written in Prolog for PC's and forms part of an *Intelligent Tutoring System* reflecting approaches currently popular in artificial intelligence research.

MacVoice helps music theory students write four-voice chorales according to practices of the seventeenth and eighteenth centuries. It was developed at Carnegie Mellon University by Marilyn Taft Thomas (Department of Music, Carnegie Mellon University, Pittsburgh, PA 15213) and others. It is distributed in the US by Kinko's Copy Shops.

Theory

Guido, developed by Fred Hofstetter on the PLATO system at the University of Delaware, includes lessons on intervals, melodies, chords, and rhythms. All are oriented towards use in ear training.

MacGamut by Ann Blombach teaches scales and other elements of music theory and analysis on the Macintosh. The program was originally designed to work with Ohio State University's Musicode 2. There is no synthesizer output. *MacGamut* is available from Mayfield Publishing Co., 1240 Villa St., Mountain View, CA 94041.

At Florida State University a broad range of music theory courseware is under development on Atari 1040 ST's. The intention is to use computer-based instructional materials, running on low-cost workstations, in all basic musicianship classes.

Sound Control and Analysis Software

CASE Sound Tools

Barry Eaglestone and others at the University of Bradford have been extending Computer Aided Software Engineering (CASE) tools to provide support for sound manipulation and synthetic musical instrument development (Computer Aided Sound Engineering). Their work is based on a Sun workstation running under UNIX. The INGRES relational database is used.

Sound Analysis

Johannes E. Philipp has developed an Interactive Signal Inspection System (ISIS) for the Atari ST. ISIS, which has been used in some ethnomusicological research, is designed to accommodated both music and speech. It provides segment labeling for pitch and duration measurement as well as rhythmic and phonetic transcription. It also provides an oscillogram display and digital-to-analog replay. Automatic pitch determination is intended. Illustrations are shown on the following page. The contact address is Beuzlen 6, D-7140 Ludwigsburg 11, Germany.

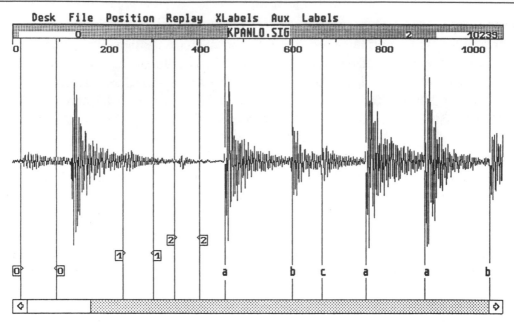

ISIS: **Comparison of membranophone and ideophone played simultaneously.**

The left side of the window shows cursor pairs (0, 1, 2) defining segments for comparison. Here they reveal that the beats within the first two segments originate from the membranophone, while the one within the third segment is a soft ideophone beat. The right side of the window shows labels (a, b, c) providing the basis for calculations of duration from one tone onset to the next.

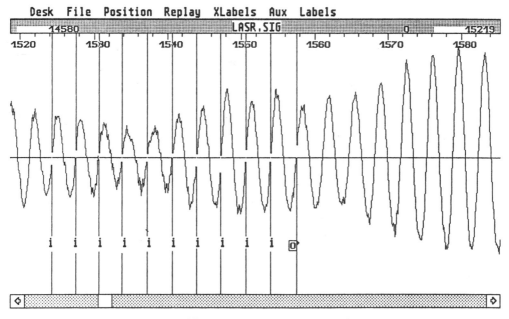

ISIS: **Oscillogram for pitch determination.**

This oscillogram is zoomed to 1280 samples per window. It facilitates the labeling of period duration for pitch determination.

Bol Processor

Version 2 of the *Bol Processor* by Bernard Bel and Jim Kippen deals with "sound objects" that may be assigned metric and topological properties. These objects are defined from prototypes, *i.e.,* musical gestures captured by an instrument and represented as sequences of MIDI messages. It runs on the Macintosh under HyperCard, permitting users to adapt the interface to their own needs. An enhanced version of the algorithmic part of BP1 is written in C. *Bols* are quasi-onomatopoeic syllables used in Indian tabla drumming. The original version of the software enabled Kippen to study improvisatory techniques in this art form and ran on the Apple IIc.

Tunings and Temperaments

Tunings and Temperaments by Igor Popovic allows users to simulate historical tunings and temperaments on an IBM PC PS/2. Eight-channel sound is output. The developer is in the Department of Music, Yale University, 143 Elm St., New Haven, CT 06510 (POPIGOA@YALEVM).

Automatic Arrangement Software

Stephen Wu's thesis research at the University of Hong Kong [see p. 18] is oriented toward the automatic arrangement of popular song melodies. In its current phase, he is developing a deterministic algorithm for rhythmic segmentation of melodies. Wu defines the rhythmic pattern as a series of pulses of sounds and silences. The best fit of a rhythm to a melody is the pattern having the minimum distance with the melody. The distance is defined after writing out both the melody and the rhythmic pattern on a time axis: for every time unit, if there is an attack point at the melody but there is none at the rhythm, or if there is no attack point at the melody but there is one at the rhythm, the distance is increased by 1. When the whole melody has been processed, the distance would have been fully accumulated. Finding the rhythm that minimizes this distance is a major challenge.

The melody is broken into two segments, to which different rhythms are assigned. These segments are checked to see if the break point is optimal and what the effect is on the overall distance. If the total distance is not optimal, this procedure becomes recursive until it is. The final rhythmic pattern is considered the best fit to the given melody.

After completing this project, Wu hopes to identify other problems of music arrangement that can be solved in a similar way.

Analysis Software

Chord Comparison

Larry J. Solomon's *Music Analysis System* software has an ever-growing range of capabilities oriented mainly towards music of the past century. The musical description is alphanumeric. The program identifies chords in the chromatic scale and tags them with set names and common chord names (when applicable). An example of its chord comparison capabilities, which include intervallic similarities, interval vector contents, and subset relations, is shown below. *MAS* also analyzes melodic series and tone rows. Input is by note name (C#, Db, etc.). A facility for MIDI input is under development.

Chord analysis by Solomon's *Music Analysis System.*

(1) Scriabin's "Prometheus" hexachord, or 6-34.
(2) Harmonic hexachord, or augmented eleventh (6-34B).
(3) Harmonic heptachord, or augmented thirteenth (7-34).

MAS can determine that (3) is a mirror-chord, that (4) is identical to (1) enharmonically, by transposition, that (1) and (2) are inversely related and are complements, and that (1), (2), and (4) are contained within (3).

An algorithm to implement Schenkerian analysis of voice-leading layers is now under development. Results can be printed with *MusicPrinter*. *MAS* is distributed by Soft Stuff Computer Co., 5122 North Tortolita Road, Tucson, AZ 85745.

Chordal/Tonal Analysis

The work of Eva Ferkova at the Czech Academy of Sciences goes well beyond chordal identification and analysis to probe such questions as how to determine starting and ending points of temporary modulation, how to discriminate between major and minor keys associated with the same key signature, and how to ascertain the contextual tonal function of a given chord. The main program considers harmonic activity on three levels—chordal, tonal, and functional. To identify temporary changes in tonality, local accidentals are tracked. The key signature can be changed by joining local accidentals to it. In evaluating chordal function in modulatory passages, the root of the current chord is compared with the root of the chord that follows.

The developers hope to extend the project to accept input from various devices and to facilitate conversion of their data format to ANSI standards. Recent programming in the project, in Turbo Pascal, has been contributed by Marian Dudek (Faculty of Mathematics and Physics, Comenius University, Bratislava). Ferkova's address is Ustav Hudobnej vedy SAV, Fajorovo nabrezie 7, 813 64 Bratislava, Czechoslovakia.

Chordal analysis of the opening movement of Beethoven's Piano Sonata Op. 78 from the project in Bratislava headed by Eva Ferkova.

Line 1 contains chord names. KA = triad; + — major; — = minor. D — dominant. Configurations are also indicated. Zm7 = 3-3-3. Zmm7 = 3-4-3. x = an ornamental tone. Line 2 contains names of tonal functions. Line 3 contains the name of the tonality. d = dur [major], m = mol [minor].

Melodic Comparison—Bevil

J. Marshall Bevil's *MelAnaly* software was originally developed in connection with a Ph.D. dissertation (North Texas State University, 1984) on British and American folk tunes. The core of the package is a menu-driven program, running on the Apple IIgs, that compares the arrays of two numerically encoded melodies in order to determine the kinship of the tunes to each other. Each melody is represented by two arrays. The first contains the codes for pitch, duration, and stress of the three-note motifs that open and close the coarse and fine strains of the melody. The second array contains pitch encoding of the complete melodic contour at three levels of details—elemental, broadly detailed, and specifically detailed. Analytical results can be displayed both graphically and statistically. An example of graphic comparison was shown in the 1988 *Directory*, pp. 119. The contact address is 4614 W. 43rd Street, Houston, TX 77092.

Melodic Comparison—Burroughs

Alexander Brinkman's binomial representation system provides the foundation for Michael Burroughs' effort at Indiana University to devise a mathematical algorithm for melodic comparison. It is a depth-first search technique that matches principal tones while ignoring inconsequential ones. Inversions and transpositions of a designated melody may be identified through linear algebraic operations.

Set-Theoretic Analysis Software

CCARH receives many reports of set-theoretic analysis programs. At this writing we are aware of approximately two dozen of them. Although we have reported on these in previous years [see the *Cumulative Index* in last year's issue], we are reluctant to list new programs unless it can be demonstrated that they contain unique capabilities and that they work with encoded music, rather than purely numeric pitch descriptions.

Software for Modelling of Music Theory

Cognitive Theories of Harmony

"New Cognitive Theories of Harmony Applied to Direct Manipulation Tools for Novices" by Simon Holland is available from the Open University as CITE Report No. 17 (1987) [address on p. 16].

Connectionist Models of Music Listening

The research of Mauri Kaipainen is directed toward an overall view of the possibilities of modelling the cognitive perceptual skills of music listening within the connectionist framework. In its first stage, it is concerned with how cognition makes use of the repetitive structures of music, with how perceptual constancies are abstracted from the acoustic continuum, how the perceptual competence can be implemented, and what the nature of the learning processes along prolonged time-intervals is. The aim of the second stage is to build a self-organizing model that extracts significant features from digitized natural sound. Kaipainen is in the Department of Musicology, University of Helsinki, Vironkatu 1, 00170 Helsinki, Finland (kaipainen@FINUH.BITNET or in% Skaipainen@ cc.helsinki.fiS).

Distributed Analysis

A program for distributed analysis of musical pieces, as proposed by Nicolas Ruwet, is under development at the Florence Conservatory by David Bencini, Michele Ignelzi, and Lelio Camilleri. This kind of analysis aims to define the formal or signifying unit (the longest unit used at least twice in a work) and its sub-units. These units acquire significance within a network of structural relationships. The user may define the parts of the signifying unit with which the analysis may be performed. The program can supply output in *SCORE* code.

The signifying unit and its repetitions in Schumann's *Canzone*.

Distributed analysis based on second half of signifying unit.

Evaluation of Predictive Theories

Darrell Conklin and Ian H. Witten are involved in an ongoing series of experiments to evaluate predictive theories of music. Initial attention is restricted to melody; testing is performed on a corpus of 100 Bach chorale melodies. Theories are evaluated by a data compression measure, which is believed to be a strong indicator of their predictive power. The entropy of the chorales is estimated by averaging the amount of compression given to a test set using a theory learned from a training set.

To date they have defined approximately 20 viewpoints, which make predictions based on duration, pitch, interval, contour, phrasing, and so forth. A distinction is made between theories that adapt to a class of sequences and those pertaining to a particular work. The authors may be contacted at the Department of Computer Science, University of Calgary, Calgary T2N 1N4, Canada.

Explication

Michael Kassler continues his research on explications of the theories of tonality proposed by A. F. C. Kollmann (1756-1828) and Heinrich Schenker. Programming is in APL on a Canon microcomputer, with output of notation files in Canon's printing system language, CaPSL [see the *1987 Directory*, p. 108]. Kassler reports that "the research differs from other projects in that it involves in-depth explication of historically important music theories rather than oversimplifications."

Fractals

In his research on modelling of compositional processes, Ioannis Zannos, who is now working at the University of Tokyo, is trying to bring a new, non-Western aesthetic perspective to the understanding of near-Eastern traditional music. In particular, he is examining the concepts of (1) fractals in relation to improvisation and (2) cellular automata in relation to the composition of polyphonic and polyrhythmic structures.

Grouping Structure

The first complete part of a Florence Conservatory expert system for music analysis is a program to implement the rules of musical grouping structures laid down by Lerdahl and Jackendoff. Current work carried out by Lelio Camilleri, Francesco Giomi, and Francesco Carreras is concerned with the development of an expert system for analytical discoveries of tonal harmonic analysis. It is based on segmentation into structurally significant time-spans at well-defined hierarchical levels. This phase of the work is being carried out in an MS DOS environment with the expert system shell *Intelligent Compiler*.

At the Open University's Institute of Educational Technology in the UK, M. Baker completed a study on "An Artificial Intelligence Approach to Musical Grouping Structure," which is available as CITE Report No. 34 [address given on p. 16].

Improvised Counterpoint

At the Massachusetts Institute of Technology Lincoln Laboratory, Timothy C. Aarset has developed, in C, a simulator of Renaissance instructions on modal counterpoint as they might have been applied in extemporaneous practice. The user may vary the rules, the order in which the rules are acquired, and the precedence of rules in cases of conflict. The musicological goal of the simulation is to demonstrate that Renaissance manuals on counterpoint contain a method for training musicians to improvise advanced florid counterpoint using the elements of hexachordal solmisation as encapsulated in the Guidonian hand. The simulation environment is based on "discrete event simulation of dynamic systems" rather than a rule-based expert system. The benefit outside Renaissance studies lies in showing how this approach can be applied generally to studies of musical processes.

Musical Intuition and Thinking

The recent work of Jeanne Bamberger in the Department of Music at the Massachusetts Institute of Technology has been especially concerned with student perception of musical structure in works from the standard repertory. Under the aegis of MIT's *Project Athena*, Bamberger developed a special language called MusicLogo, which is related to LISP. Because MIDI-compatible music primitives are incorporated, students have simultaneous access to as many as four voices, a wide selection of timbral "instrument" settings, and extensive procedural control of material. The students are given design constraints within which to work. The hardware environment, which includes four IBM PC AT's and ten Macintoshes, is complemented by a *Sourcebook* and an *Athena Music Workbook* written by Bamberger.

One way of working with this system is to listen to a piece of music, describe it procedurally, and then attempt to create a new piece of music conforming to the procedure. Overwhelmingly, students have found that there is a large gap between perceived procedure and a complete description and that even intellectually simple procedural descriptions can generate perceptually complex music.

In relation to the discovery that Vivaldi's music cannot be reduced to procedural generalization, Bamberger writes that the research "gives pause to notions of what the computer is and is not good for: Rather than a medium that can substitute for thinking, listening, and playing music on real musical instruments, or even make such activities easier, the computer becomes a medium through which to interrogate and challenge one's everyday knowledge so as to build on it. In this way the Lab serves not as a source of answers, but rather as an environment for moving towards a better understanding of how learning happens."

Style Simulation

Experiments in Musical Intelligence (EMI) is an ongoing research project conducted by David Cope at the University of California at Santa Cruz to simulate well defined musical styles of classical composers, twentieth-century styles, and certain ethnic repertories. The experiments are based on classical pattern-matching techniques used in artificial intelligence. Its working metaphor is linguistic: a rule-base structures the voicing constraints and new works are composed top-down. *EMI*'s working library includes simulated Bach two-part inventions, Mozart keyboard sonatas (one movement), Bartok *Mikrokosmos*, and Palestrina four-voice compositions.

Some of the factors considered in creating a stylistic profile are the maximum number of pitches allowed in a motive, the overall time length of a motive, constraints on melodic shape, level of dissonance, key shifts, and variation by augmentation, diminution, inversion, and ornamentation.

When a second work is analyzed and a subsequent image is overlaid on the first, those motives which significantly increase in number are considered to be the essence of the style of the composer. The locations of these motives, which are now called *signatures*, are noted for the framework of future compositions. Those that increase somewhat are considered *coercing agents*. The remaining material is considered local to each work and is discarded from the profile. Cope is currently writing a book on *Computers and Musical Style* for the A-R Digital Audio Series.

Theories of Musical Information

Number-Line Representations of Pitch

Walter B. Hewlett, the director of CCARH, will present a description of his system for representing the letter name, octave number, and accidental applied to a note as a single parameter, for use in the analysis of tonal music at the conference on Computers in Music Research in 1991.

An Object-Oriented Approach to Musical Information

Alan Marsden (The Queen's University, Belfast) probes the applicability of object-oriented data definitions to music-analytic applications in a forthcoming publication. In object-oriented programming, data types which are conceptually similar but technically different may be available for linked or hierarchically prioritized operations.

A Data Structure for Score Representation

John William Schaffer (University of Wisconsin) advocates the use of a data structure for score representation and analysis that takes advantage of Prolog's support for predicates and list structures in a talk scheduled for presentation to the Society of Music Theory in Oakland in November 1990.

Composition and Music Systems Software

APL for Music

APL for Music (an extension of the IBM mainframe language called A Programming Language) is a multifaceted computer music system under development by Stanley Jordan. It provides support for algorithmic composition, computer-assisted music instruction, granular synthesis, MIDI score editing, and music theory and analysis. A description of the system is included in the Association of Computing Machinery's *APL89 Conference Proceedings*, which is available from Jordan at 163 Third Ave., Ste. 143, New York, NY 10003, and as #554890 from the ACM Order Department, Waverly Press, PO Box 64145, Baltimore, MD 21264.

"Musical Syntactic and Semantic Structures in APL2" is the title of a paper by Jordan and Erik S. Friis scheduled to appeared in the ACM *APL90 Conference Proceedings*. The authors describe their system for using general arrays to represent syntactic information in the form of MIDI data streams and illustrate a semantic structure by defining a diatonic scale. Chords are created within the scale using the "each" operator. Copies may be requested from Friis, IBM Corp., Route 100, Somers, NY 10589.

The Composers' Desktop Project

The Composers' Desktop Project is an independent, non-profit limited company which is distinct from but closely in touch with York University. Enquiries may be addressed to Martin Atkins, Composers' Desktop Project Ltd., Unit 7, 35 Hospital Fields Rd., Fulford Industrial Estate, York YO1 4DZ, UK (44-904-613299) [see p. 128].

Keynote

Keynote is a UNIX-based programming language for manipulating and generating music with MIDI-compatible equipment. It was designed as an application-specific language and interactive shell by Tim Thompson at AT&T Bell Labs. Although support for algorithmic composition was a central goal, *Keynote* also serves as a utility for non-realtime and realtime data manipulation. Nested pop-up menus and operations of a graphical music editor have been implemented. The AT&T UNIX Toolchest contains source code for *Keynote*; binaries for the Macintosh and Amiga are also available. Modest licensing fees are charged for both the Toolchest and *Keynote*. A reference manual is available from Thompson, AT&T Bell Labs, Room 3C-231, Crawford's Corner Road, Holmdel, NJ 07733 (tjt@twitch.att.com). A user group has recently been organized by Jon W. Backstrom, Applied Digital Arts, PO Box 176, Bloomington, IN 47401-0176 (media@silver.ucs.indiana.edu). A quarterly newsletter is available by subscription.

Music4C

Music4C is a sound synthesis and signal processing program in C for the Macintosh. It includes source code in THINK C and is available from Graeme Gerrard, Faculty of Music, University of Melbourne, Royal Parade, Parkville 3052, Australia.

Ravel

Ravel is an interpreted music programming language resembling C. It runs on the IBM PC/MPU-401. Data can be imported from MIDI files and from *Cakewalk*, a popular sequencer program. *Ravel* is in the public domain. Details of a jazz improvisation program written in the language are available from James Binkley, 5814 S. W. Taylor, Portland, OR 97221.

Symbolic Composer

Symbolic Composer, written in LISP, uses symbol and vector patterns to describe the elements of composition. The software makes it possible to use any information structure (for example, from astronomy or organic chemistry) as a seed to produce music. The basic idea of the software is total freedom of conversion between symbolic and numeric information.

Melodies, harmonies, velocities, lengths and "humanizing parameters" are described separately for each instrument. They may be constructed manually or with generators. Symbol generators are based on recursive association structures. There is also a Fibonacci string generator. The software runs on the Atari ST. It can also control three-dimensional objects and S-geometry animations on a Symbolics workstation. Resulting MIDI files can be used with *Masterscore*. A manual in English is currently in preparation. Further information and demonstration cassettes may be requested from Pekka Tolonen, Frederikinkatu 26 D 40, SF-00120 Helsinki, Finland.

Workstations and Integrated Projects

Berkeley: CNMAT

At the Center for New Music and Audio Technologies, a part of the University of California at Berkeley, Adrian Freed directs the program in New Media Resources for Music Scholarship and Education. One of the project's goals is to develop with readily available and affordable components workstations that serve music scholars. Conceived in a hypermedia environment, such systems would provide rapid access to suitably indexed audio materials, representations of notated music, text materials, and images.

In related work, Ben Brinner is developing an *Ethnomusicologist's Workbench* to aid in the exploration and characterization of recorded materials. This environment consists of tools for selecting, playing, viewing, editing, and transcribing segments of recorded performance. These tools are complemented by a signal processing library with procedures for pitch extraction, temporal segmentation, and separation of simultaneous sound sources.

Other avenues of research at CNMAT include projects in computer architectures for sound synthesis and research on music perception and cognition, especially in relation to traditional approaches to music theory and composition. In the first case, significant design work, under the direction of John Wawrzynek, has taken place for a Memory Intensive Music Integrated Circuit (MIMIC). David Wessel heads the effort in cognition and perception and is research director of the Center. Richard Felciano is the general director of CNMAT. Enquiries may be addressed to any of the above at 1750 Arch St., Berkeley, CA 94720.

Boston University

Otto Laske proposes that a musicological workstation linking an interactive music environment, an automated composition module, and tools for modelling musical knowledge acquisition should be developed. Ideally it would provide hypermedia facilities for using notated scores in modelling knowledge and would permit musical sounds to become part of the material for modelling by using video disk. He encourage readers interested in such a project to contact him at 926 Greendale Avenue, Needham, MA 02191 (laske@bu-cs.bu.edu or 617-449-0781).

Florence Conservatory

The Teletau system of musical encoding, processing, and playback developed in the 1970's and early 80's on mainframe computers at C.N.U.C.E. in Pisa is currently being adapted to the MS DOS environment under the direction of Lelio Camilleri at the Florence Conservatory in cooperation with I.R.O.E., another institute of the Centro Nazionale di Ricerca in Pisa.

The aim of this project is to provide a musical workstation with all the flexible features of the original Teletau system in combination with conversion routines to commercially available software for microcomputers. Micro-Teletau will provide programs for encoding, processing, and playback (eight-voice polyphony), a library of encoded pieces, and transcoding support for the creation of *SCORE* print files. Because of the absence of a graphical interface, support for blind and visually limited users is intended. The software development work is being carried out by Camilleri, Francesco Giomi, Paolo Graziani, and Lucia Taggi, with a view towards completion by the end of 1990.

Milan: LIM

The research coordinated by Goffredo Haus on the development of an *Intelligent Music Workstation* is carried out at the Laboratorio di Informatica Musicale at the University of Milan. Including collaborators from the artificial intelligence and music labs at the Universities of Genoa (D.I.S.T.) and Padua (C.S.C.), there are now ten researchers and 20 graduate students working on various aspects of the project. The goal of the project is to design and develop a musical software and hardware environment in which commercially available products can be integrated with prototypical modules built within the context of musical informatics research. Funding has been provided by the Italian National Research Council through the end of 1992.

The *Intelligent Music Workstation* is an open environment, so that musicians can add their own applications. Most modules run on the Macintosh family of computers. All software modules are able to import and export standard MIDI files in three available formats. Sound files are compatible with the Digidesign Sound Designer format. A HyperText interface is provided.

Modules currently in preparation provide such capabilities as the following:

- Editing and synthesis of sound samples
- Hybrid environments for knowledge representations based on Petri nets
- HyperText retrieval of sampled sounds in a 7000-item data base
- An expert system for piano-bar-like improvisation
- Musical object segmentation routines for fugue and sonata form
- Audiovisual performance combining MIDI processes with automatic generation of Escher-like tessellations

No coding format for the symbolic level of information has been adopted yet, but serious attention is being given to ANSI *SMDL* [see *Technical Standards*].

Most of the modules will be available free of charge, for academic use only, at the end of 1992. Those interested may contact the director at L.I.M., Dipartimento di Scienze dell'Informazione, Università degli Studi, via Moretto da Brescia 9, I-20133 Milan, Italy (MUSIC@IMISIAM.BITNET).

University of Amsterdam

In the Center for Experimental Music at the University of Amsterdam a broad range of applications is being supported with a diverse array of commercial hardware and software. Macintosh computers are being used for MIDI applications; printing applications are carried out with *Finale*. Atari Mega ST's are being used for more elaborate projects, sometimes involving the Composers' Desktop system [see p. 123], to run *CSound*, *CMusic*, and the *Phase Vocoder*. For general musicological applications the *Note Processor* is being used on IBM PC's.

Three dissertations in the department relate to experimental music. One, recently completed by Christiane ten Hoopen, concerns form and structure in electroacoustic music. One on voice synthesis will include a survey of current systems and potential applications in this area. Another concerns simulation of formalized systems, including those of Xenakis, and interactive improvisation. Leigh Landy directs the Center, which is located at Spuistraat 134, 1012 VB Amsterdam, The Netherlands (LSNDY@ALF. LET.UVA.NL). Leo Plenckers supervises applications in historical and ethnomusicology.

University of Wisconsin

The *Composer's Studio* project at the University of Wisconsin involves the integration of a variety of software to provide a flexible working environment for a composer on a NeXT workstation. The facilities available will include notation and audio synthesis as well as a framework for the representation of manipulation of compositional information at a variety of hierarchical and theoretical levels. Currently a model for the representation of musical knowledge is under development; a note-list approach has been deemed inadequate. Stephen Dembski (School of Music, University of Wisconsin, 455 N. Park St., Madison, WI 53706) directs the project. Edith Epstein, a doctoral student in Computer Science, is his assistant.

Data

Data Bases of Text:
Approaches to Organization and Access

In previous years we have provided detailed listings of a large number of data base projects, most of which are still running. Readers may consult the comprehensive index in the 1989 edition of *Computing in Musicology* to locate information about these projects. The need for a comprehensive bibliographical list of data base projects maintained by both individuals and groups has been recognized by the International Musicological Society's Study Group on Musical Data. In this issue we turn the focus temporarily to issues of organization, dissemination, and access relevant to all data bases. Projects that illustrate the issues discussed are cited. Readers are urged to continue reporting their work for inclusion in future issues.

Data bases form a central pool of information for an increasing number of scholarly collaborations. Working groups attempting to establish guidelines for new data bases confront many issues in common, irrespective of whether they are international collaborations or desktop projects. Such questions as (1) whether the data is raw or interpreted, (2) whether it is complete ("fulltext") or selected ("structured"), (3) whether it is intended to generate a printed result and/or to support online searching, and (4) whether it is fixed and final or a bank of information that is periodically updated differentiate one kind of data base from another. In addition to the general issues of organization that all data bases face, the nature of the topic may provide opportunities and raise issues of its own. We have attempted to underscore these considerations in the following discussion.

Fulltext Data Bases

A fulltext data base is a machine transcription, or encoding, or a complete work or works. Shakespeare's plays offer an illustrative example. Encodings of different editions are currently available from at least four sources—a commercial software firm (CMC Research, Inc., 7150 Southwest Hampton, Suite C-120, Portland, OR 97223), an academic press (Oxford University Press), an academic computing service (the Oxford Text Archives), and a hardware manufacturer (NeXT, Inc.). The range of choices available to those seeking an online Shakespeare may be suggestive of choices that will someday be available for musical repertories and treatises. For scholars, the question right now is often, "Is this possible?" In a few years it could well be, "Which source do I want to use?"

Fulltext data bases can be created by keyboarding or by optical scanning. The latter technology is more labor-intensive than many project planners realize, since data verification can be more arduous than for ordinary typescript. Scanning errors tend to be very subtle ones that are neither easily recognized by the naked eye nor anticipated on the basis of experience with text created by typists. Optical scanning produces an electronic facsimile. [Discussion of the technical aspects of optical scanning occurs on pp. 36-7. Keyboarding provides many choices for encoding.

Technical facility supports much that existing copyright law does not allow, and this gap is the most serious issue confronting scholars wishing to develop fulltext data bases. In the case of fulltext data bases, recent scholarship that already exists in published form is less likely to be made available for electronic distribution than works from the nineteenth and earlier centuries, even when the new work has been created from an electronic manuscript. Since this problem is broadly relevant to electronic publishing, it is more likely to be resolved in the commercial sphere than in the academic one. Yet scholars need to take cognizance of it.

Fulltext data bases exist in the first instance without support software. When such data bases are distributed commercially, they are often bundled with software that permits structured searches of specified kinds. Despite the completeness of the text, users may not be able to make up their own questions or to browse through or print large portions of the text. Such restrictions, when imposed by the software, protect the developer's investment of time in creating and correcting the text but may limit its potential uses. To put these considerations in perspective, we are profiling below two projects directed toward similar goals of encoding of medieval music treatises. These projects are called *THEMA* and the *Thesaurus Musicarum Latinarum*.

THEMA

THEMA is a textual data base of more than two megabytes developed by a single individual, Sandra Pinegar, in the context of research for a doctoral dissertation. It comprises music-theoretical texts in Latin of the thirteenth and fourteenth centuries. Many of the treatises are anonymous and most are not exactly dated. It is illustrative of efforts to capture raw data electronically.

Texts of this period are highly abbreviated and a system of encoding abbreviations by two-digit "tags" is a unique part of *THEMA*, which is designed to reflect the actual appearance of the text as well as to convey the text itself. This encoding system allows determination of the density of abbreviation in a source and documentation of changes of abbreviations from one gathering to another. It can aid in tracing some scribal errors to misreadings of abbreviated words found in other exemplars. Even changes from gathering to gathering can be examined. Approximately three dozen works by such figures (or hands) as Walter Odington, Magister Franciscus, Jerome of Moravia, and Anonymous IV have so far been encoded.

THEMA is readily transportable for use in a variety of word processing and concordance programs and for use with a variety of hardware configurations. It has been developed in an MS-DOS environment. Because it forms an integral part of dissertation research, methods of distributing the data to other scholars have not been a primary concern. In principle, however, the emphasis is on creating an electronic transcription that, once verified, will remain fixed. Enquiries about *THEMA* may be addressed to Sandra Pinegar, Music Department, Dodge Hall 703, Columbia University, New York, NY 10027.

THESAURUS MUSICARUM LATINARUM

The *Thesaurus Musicarum Latinarum*, a collaborative project led by Thomas J. Mathiesen at Indiana University, is intended to include fulltext encodings of all music theory treatises in Latin from the sixth through the mid-sixteenth centuries.

Previously encoded materials in Greek and Latin have been amalgamated with optically scanned nineteenth-century editions by Coussemaker and Gerbert to produce a first phase of data capture. It is hoped that the project will eventually include the series *Corpus Scriptorum de Musica, Divitiae musicae artis*, the Colorado College Critical Texts, and unedited manuscript sources. This project is illustrative of the use of edited and interpreted data, since it incorporates modern transcriptions and requires regularizations of presentation and typography.

In the *TML* spellings are normalized, diacriticals are omitted, abbreviations are expanded, and proper nouns are capitalized. Musical symbols will be entered according to a table of alphanumeric codes that include shapes of notes and ligatures, coloration, mensuration and proportion signs, and so forth. In contrast to most of the encoding schemes for early notation discussed earlier [pp. 23-35], this approach is a text-oriented one stressing the identity of each object but not expressing the relationship between objects. It is highly specific, however, distinguishing, for example, between a square flat sign ("sqb") and a rounded one ("rob").

Eventual distribution through a mainframe-based online listserver at Indiana University is the current goal. The intended uses are to facilitate studies of terminology and the preparation of concordances and new critical editions, which in turn can become part of the data base. The *TML*'s address is Dept. of Music, School of Music, Indiana University, Bloomington, IN 47405 (MATHIESE@IUBACS.BITNET or MATHIESE@ UCS.INDIANA.EDU).

Structured Data Bases

The material in a structured data base has been selected and organized in some way to facilitate its use. Structured data bases include those created with commercial relational data base software, such as dBase III or ORACLE. Structured data bases suit many kinds of subject matter. In particular we have reported a large number of projects concerned with cataloguing instruments by type or location and with cataloguing repertories. Several data bases devoted to repertorial histories of opera (the Verdi project at New York University, the Puccini project at the Technical University in Berlin, work at the Wagner Archives in Munich) are also under development. Generally these data bases are constructed and maintained by one or a few individuals. The largest and best known relational data bases are bibliographical ones developed and maintained by library consortia; we reported extensively on three of these—RISM, RLIN, and OCLC—in our 1988 issue [pp. 11-32]. Since structured data bases require user selection of material, the copyright inherently lies with the person who constructs the data base. The central questions concerning structured data bases are what to include, how to arrange and record the information, and how to disseminate the data. It is really methods of dissemination that most readily distinguish different categories of data bases. For large bibliographical data bases, the current direction is toward distribution on CD-ROM. Some representative examples from the field of music are the following:

■ MUSIC CATALOGUE OF THE NETHERLANDS (MCN). The *Music Catalogue of the Netherlands* sells its catalogue of 200,000 comprehensive title descriptions of printed music, in principle allowing every detail to be retrieved on a CD-ROM with system messages for IBM-PC compatible machines in English and Dutch. Enquiries may be sent to MCN MUSICROM, Postbus 119, 1200 AC Hilversum, The Netherlands.

■ OCLC. The Online Computer Library Center, Inc. is offering two sets of bibliographical records on CD-ROM. One set facilitates cataloguing while the other supports reference searching. Both are part of the *CAT CD450* system, a desktop reference library of bibliographical data bases. The *Music Cataloguing Collection* contains records for nearly one million sound recordings and music scores in one alphabetical file on two discs. The sound recordings data base, called Music Library, is also separately available in a format that permits queries for individual works and supports customization of records. It is based on more than 400,000 citations from US libraries. The contact address is OCLC, 6565 Frantz Road, Dublin, OH 43017-0702.

■ OLIS. *OLIS*, an orchestral repertory data base listing more than 4000 titles, is built in *Advanced Revelation* and operates on IBM PC's. It includes information about artists, contracts, concert attendance, and premières. Developed originally for in-house use by the American Symphony Orchestra League, OLIS has been made available as a bibliographical resource. Enquiries may be sent to OLIS, 777-14th St. NW, Washington, DC 20005 (202-628-0099).

■ RILM. A CD-ROM containing the entire contents of *RILM* from 1970 through 1984 is scheduled for release in the autumn of 1990 by the National Information Services Corp. Seventy thousand abstracts from more than 300 music journals will reside on the disk, which is available by subscription. Periodic updates and annual reissues are planned. Information is available from Fred Durr, 6, Wyman Tower, 3100 St. Paul St., Baltimore, MD 21218 (301-243-0797).

The distribution of individually maintained data bases has been inhibited in recent years by lack of compatibility between commercial data base programs and by the absence of recognized conduits for distribution. The first obstacle has been resolved by the software industry. The second is being redressed in the sciences and in business applications, as large clusters of data on related topics but in diverse formats are assembled in more general formats, with appropriate search tools, on CD-ROM's.

Multi-use and Unpublished Data Bases

Publishing technology is increasingly supportive of data distribution in multiple formats. The content consists of complete texts or selected information. A hardcopy publication in the sciences may also be available (although at considerable expense) as a set of graphic images of the pages on a CD-ROM. These images (constituting an electronic facsimile) are viewable but not machine-searchable. The two sets of information remain identical.

Some authors and publishers are also supporting dual modes of publication consisting of a hardcopy product in fixed form and a machine-readable source that is periodically updated. One example is provided by Charles Mould's dBaseIII+ information bank on keyboard instrument makers. Mould's immediate objective was to create copy for the third edition of D. H. Boalch's *Makers of the Harpsichord and Clavichord, 1440-1840*. The conventional book is scheduled for publication in 1991 by Oxford University Press, but scholars will also be able to gain access to a periodically updated data base, which currently lists more than 350 instruments not described in the second edition.

In other cases there may be hardcopy and electronic complements to the same set of information. This is the case with Robert M. Keller's *Dance Figures Index: American Country Dances, 1730-1810*. The figures of 2738 dances have been encoded (for example, OXR = "Circle, Hands across, Right and Left") and are listed by title, by figure, and by page location in a book of 120 pages (ISBN 1-887984-04-3). The data itself is available in dBase or IBM DOS text-file format on a companion diskette (1-

877984-05-1). Both items are available at modest cost from the Henrickson Group, PO Box 766, Sandy Hook, CT 06482.

In some cases the original purpose of the data base is to facilitate the creation of indices that are in turn designed to facilitate access to original source material, so they are concerned with information on two levels--the data immediately available and the sources on which this is based. The *Register of Musical Data in London Newspapers, 1660-1800*, which is based at Royal Holloway and Bedford New College, aims to facilitate extraction of all musical references contained in London newspapers by organizing and indexing them. It uses the ORACLE database management system with the query language SQL. Key word searching and free access to the text base are both supported. Further information is available from Rosamund McGuinness, Dept. of Music, Royal Holloway and Bedford New College, Egham Hill, Egham, Surrey TW20 0EX, UK.

Data bases designed to provide access via a personal computer to bibliographical information are proliferating in countries in which telephone access charges are not prohibitive. Such means of access are the intended mode of operation for such US projects as *Jazzbank*, a discographical data base under development by David Robinson Jr. on the ORACLE relational data base management system, and the *Union Catalog of Black Music Holdings* developed by Samuel A. Floyd Jr. with the STAR data base and information retrieval systems.

Syntagma Musicum, a bibliographical data bank of recently published musicological articles based in Turin, Italy, is unusual in that it permits users to type in messages to other users and to make information of their own available. The main entries are assembled monthly from periodicals available at the Della Corte Civic Library. Publications seeking inclusion may be sent to the Istituto di Musica Antica Pamparato, via Gioverti 75, I-10128 Turin, Italy, with a request to open a free subscription. Schematic classification follows RISM guidelines. Entries are kept as short as possible. The data bank can be reached by telephone (modem) at 011-39-59-62-75. The data bank is supported by the city government. No special software is required. User access is free.

The creation of in-house catalogues with potential for multiple methods of distribution constitutes a perennially important sphere of activity. Among newly reported projects, that of the Centro de Documentacion Musical de Andalucía (Carrera de Darro, 29, 18010 Granada, Spain) will interest those engaged in the study of Spanish music. It is concerned with the music and dance of Andalucia and extends to inventories of original musical sources, modern editions, recordings, and instruments. The collection of this information will facilitate the creation of an encyclopedia of music and dance in the province and will also provide a basis for future editions and recordings.

MusikkFUNN: A Music Network

Nothing reported in this section matches the ambitious plans for *MusikkFUNN*, a music information network intended for operation within the FUNN framework supported by the government of Norway. Fourteen FUNN centers have been designated. They will serve individuals, schools, research centers, business and industry, and the public sector. Each center will provide information services for its own geographical region. The intention is to provide facilities that, because they are of the highest quality, would be prohibitively expensive for most enterprises to maintain individually.

MusikkFUNN, as conceived by its originators at the Western Norway Research Centre, will provide access to bibliographical information [taking as its model the *Musiek Catalogus Nederland*; see p. 134], address lists for amateur and professional musicians, tools for the preparation of concert programs, and optical disk storage of musical scores. Links with a proposed National Centre of Music Technology, coordinated by Arvid Vollsnes of the University of Oslo, are also intended. An associated data base of documents relating to the life and music of Edvard Grieg [see pp. 153-4] is currently in preparation at Sogndal College of Education. Further particulars may be obtained from Dagfinn Bach, Project Manager, MusikkFUNN, Vestlandsforsking, Fjørevegen 17, P.B. 163, 5801 Sogndal, Norway.

Data Bases including Musical Incipits

Data bases of musical incipits involve the encoding of musical information together with bibliographical records that provide information about the source. They can be designed for any of the kinds of dissemination mentioned above, although the possibility of corruption in direct electronic transmission poses serious problems to data integrity.

The most extensive bank of encoded musical incipits is that maintained by RISM in Frankfurt for the indexing of seventeenth- and eighteenth-century manuscripts of European music. More than 100,000 incipits and associated bibliographical data can now be retrieved by personal computer. RISM's data is designed to facilitate the creation of catalogues of sources. These have already taken the form of hardcopy books devoted to the holdings of one library and microfiches of aggregate sources. Other methods of access and dissemination may occur in the future. RISM's musical data, which was described in the 1988 *Directory*, is encoded in Plaine and Easie. A facility for screen display of musical information has recently been developed at the project's central headquarters in Frankfurt and is to be used by French and English working groups. Further information is available in *INFO RISM* No. 2 (April 1990), pp. 7-17, and from RISM-Zentralredaktion, Sophienstr. 26, D-6000 Frankfurt/M. 90 (069-70-62-31).

Another ambitious project, in terms of the quantity of information involved, is the National Tune Index series, which is concerned with providing linked title and letter-code music listing of tens of thousands of British and American works (songs, dances, ballad operas, wind band music et al.) of earlier centuries. The quantity of information is immense, and the listings are currently provided on microfiche through University Music Editions (P.O. Box 192, Fort George Stations, New York, NY 10040). A guidebook by the project's originators and directors, Kate Van Winkle Keller and Carolyn Rabson, is also available. NTI data consists of pitch and stress information and is cross-referenced by incipits given in scale degrees, incipits given in stressed-note sequence, and incipits given in interval sequence as well as by titles, tune names, first lines, and so forth.

Many individual data bases of musical incipit information are developed to support the creation of thematic indices. In relation to catalogues of repertory, two of the biggest undertakings—Harry Lincoln's *Italian Madrigal Indexes* and Jan LaRue's *Thematic Identifier* for his *Catalogue of 18th-Century Symphonies*—have recently come to fruition. Lincoln's catalogue, published by Yale University Press in 1989 is now the model for a sixteenth-century motet index. It provides the music itself and various indices, such as an intervallic sequence index, in the same volume. LaRue's work, planned for three volumes, provides a letter-code thematic locator in the first volume (Indiana University Press, 1989); musical material will follow in ensuing volumes.

Musical Data

MAPPET from Essen University

The most significant release of musical data suited to academic use over the past year has been of folk materials encoded over many years at Essen University in Germany. These materials, consisting mainly of German and Chinese songs, have all been encoded in *ESAC*, the Essen Associative Code. This is an alphanumeric scheme for the representation of pitch and duration. Lyrics are not included.

The *LIED* and *BALL* data bases of German folk materials contain approximately 6000 melodies. The *ETHNO* data base contains information on approximately 4000 works from many cultures available on sound recordings. The *LIAO* data base combines features of the other data bases in that it contains information on 1500 recorded Chinese folk songs, and it contains encoded melodies for almost 800 of these. *ETHNOBIB* and *EDVLIT* are bibliographical data bases citing books and articles on ethnomusicology (537 items) in the first case and computer applications in music (1113 items) in the second. DIAS contains short descriptions of 1573 slides related to music in the Peoples' Republic of China. *ICTM* lists 47 projects (through January 1990) of the International Council on Traditional Music involving computers. The data bases are available in AskSam and ASCII format.

MAPPET is a package of support software for using and in fact extending the musical data bases. It provides for MIDI input, editing, and storage, detects syntax errors, and supports playback and analysis (intervals, scale degrees, patterns). It also permits searches of all the data bases on a single command. Translations of ESAC code into standard MIDI (written in C for the Atari series of microcomputers), into RELAM (real-time MIDI), and into DARMS. *AskSam* queries can be accessed in English, German, French, Italian, and Swedish. The manual is available in German and in Peter Cooke's English translation.

Data and software are available by license at minimal cost from Prof. Dr. Helmut Schaffrath, Universität Essen, FB 4 - Musik - Postfach 4300 Essen 1, Germany. Two provisions of the license agreement are that additions and corrections by users be made available for inclusion in updated versions of the data bases and that the source of the data be acknowledged in publications.

Music Data from Passport Designs

Passport Designs, a commercial music software company, launched a new Music Data division in the spring of 1990. Its initial release consisted of twelve digitized repertories of professionally recorded, "presequenced" music. Works can be arranged and orchestrated for playback on MIDI equipment. The main emphasis is on popular repertories including jazz, country and Western music, rhythm and blues, and big band performances, but some classical works, including Bach's Brandenburg Concertos, are also available. *MIDI Hits* are available in Macintosh, Atari ST, and IBM PC formats. Further information is available from Music Data, 625 Miramontes Street, Half Moon Bay, CA 94019 (415-726-0280).

MusicWriter Musical Data Distribution System

This MusicWriter [in contrast to *The Portable Musicwriter*, a dedicated system for printing music that is listed on p. 70] is a support system for the distribution of encoded music on CD-ROM. The data is intended for distribution to music stores, where consumers can customize material for on-demand printing via commercial programs for music printing. Pieces can be auditioned before purchase. An alternative use of the data is to create a MIDI diskette for use on a home synthesizer. Amiga, Atari, IBM PC, and Macintosh formats are all supported. Further information is available from Jon Monday, MusicWriter, Inc., 21569 Mary Alice Way, Los Gatos, CA 95030 (408-353-2225).

Hyperware and Hybrid Products

Interactive CD's

Hypermedia products involve the linking of diverse kinds of information. HyperCard capabilities for the Macintosh have spawned dozens of specific applications for teaching and bibliography. The possibilities supported by HyperCard when linked with sound recordings and/or MIDI instruments have given rise to a new kind of teaching tool—the interactive compact disk (CD+I).

Robert Winter's *CD Companion to Beethoven's Ninth Symphony* was released in November 1989 by the Voyager Company. The *Companion*, which assumes no detailed knowledge of music, provides a lot of text information about Beethoven's life and times and a glossary of terms as well as commentary on the music. Musical notation and corresponding sound are coupled. The software is on computer diskettes, the music on a standard CD.

A similar idea is pursued by Warner New Media's *Audio Notes* series, in which the first offering, Mozart's *Magic Flute*, was published in March 1990. In this case the original recording and support materials are on the same CD's. These materials include digitized musical examples and commentary, plot synopses, and libretti in both English and German that move at the same speed as the music on systems that include a CD+Graphics player. *Audio Notes* products can also drive a laser videodisk player, and *The Magic Flute* (which occupies three CD's) can be synchronized with an Ingmar Bergman production on disk. Beethoven's String Quartet No. 14 was released in September. Partly because of the inclusion of thousands of digitized pictures, the product requires 6.5 megabytes of free space on a hard disk.

Both firms have a series of releases scheduled. Warner's list includes Brahms's *German Requiem*, Stravinsky's *Rite of Spring*, Berlioz's *Symphonie Fantastique*, and Beethoven's Seventh Symphony as well as jazz and popular titles. Voyager has also announced a *Rite of Spring*.

In a review in *Notes* (47/1 [1990], 91-7), Karl Miller writes that the *CD Companion* "is a guide to the power of media in the learning environment....It is most significant that this program was prepared by a musicologist who lays no claim to great facility with computers....[The] relative ease of construction [of CD+I tools] will likely stimulate the development of many similar packages."

Robert Skinner reviews laser videodisks—notably the Voyager Company's earlier *Bachdisc*, a series of performances of and commentary on the B-Minor Fugue from Part Two of *The Well-Tempered Clavier* by Juan Downey, and the University of Delaware's

---

Videodisk Music Series, a collection of recordings with scrolling scores and background material prepared by Fred T. Hofstetter—in *Notes* 46/1 (1989), 104-8.

Hypermedia Data Bases and Teaching Tools

Country Blues in Hypermedia

Adrian Freed at CNMAT, Berkeley, has been developing a data base of *Country Blues in Hypermedia*. It incorporates text, pictures, and sound. Each text line of every song is indexed to the appropriate point on the recording (scores are not indexed). Most of the sound material is from 78 rpms. The authoring platform consists of a Macintosh computer, HyperCard, SoundBase, and a Dyaxis hard disk recording system. The Dyaxis system (from Studer Editech, 1370 Willow Road, Menlo Park, CA 94025) facilitates the transfer of sound material to a hard disk. A set of external command modules was used to control the Dyaxis sound playback from HyperCard.

Music Cultures of the World

At the University of Southern California, Gilbert Blount, Charlotte Crockett, and William Alves are creating a multimedia text entitled *Musical Cultures of the World*. Written on a HyperText platform, *Musical Cultures* provides access to a glossary of terms, bibliographical material, a picture library stored on an interactive videodisk, and a sound library on an interactive CD.

Dedicated Applications

Antiquities

Deciphering the Ugaritic Musical Notation

David Halperin of Tel-Aviv University reports that he is currently working on the decipherment of the Ugaritic musical notation. [Ugarit is the oldest known site of human habitation in Syria. Its civilization, which can be dated back to the fifth millennium, reached its peak in the fifteenth and fourteen centuries B.C. Poetic works of the Canaanites are recorded in Ugaritic.] The earliest known written music is that found in the excavations of the Royal Palace at Ras Shamrah. The notational "words" are Hurrian adaptations of terms known from Mesopotamian cuneiform tablets which deal with music theory. In the Mesopotamian tablets, the terms which parallel the Ugaritic ones are names for pairs of strings, or possibly for the intervals formed by pairs of strings.

The realization of the Ugaritic-Hurrian "words" (be they notes or tablature) in modern notation remains problematic. All decipherments so far made have been unsatisfactory, some even to their own authors. These attempts all assume that phonetically similar terms have semantically similar meanings—an assumption which requires proof, when one considers the separation in space and time between the Ugaritic and the Mesopotamian civilizations [the boundaries of Mesopotamia are included in modern Iraq]. It would be of value to have an objective and independent confirmation or rejection of the connection by the use of a quasi-cryptographic method, which ultimately generates what is known to statisticians as a seriation.

The "words" are assumed to be names of notes. These notes are assumed to have an underlying re-entrant order, which is the Ugaritic scale. The literary texts accompanying the notation are assumed to have no influence on the pitches of the scale. And the crucial assumption is that the notated melodies will tend to show a preference for conjunct motion.

Eleven different "words" are first listed in some arbitrary order. This list is then subjected to all possible permutations; as there are eleven different "words," some 40 million (factorial 11) are available. For each permutation, the distance for each pair of "words" is determined from a metric which is a function of the linear separation between the two "words" involved within the current permutation. Then, for each permutation, a calculation is made of the total "distance" found between adjacent "words" in all of the tablets and fragments. Finally, that permutation which yields the smallest total distance is chosen as being the one which represents the order of the notes in the Ugaritic scale.

The scale thus determined provides no indication as to which is the ascending direction, but the additional assumption of a tendency to prefer a descending melodic line can compensate for this lack. Also undetermined is the intervallic content of the scale, for which the method used has no answer. Nevertheless, an experimental transcription of the complete hymn-tune found in one of the tablets produces a melody which seems to make sense.

The ordering produced by the procedure turns out to be essentially the same as that found in certain of the Mesopotamian instrument-tuning texts. The affinity thus demonstrated appears to justify the assumptions made; and the scale order found can therefore serve as a starting point for future attempts at decipherment.

Renaissance and Baroque Music

The Madrigals of Luca Bati

A critical edition of the madrigals of Luca Bati, a late-Renaissance composer from Florence, is currently being prepared by Piero Gargiulo at the Florence Conservatory using *SCORE*. The works will be published by the firm of Olschki in Florence in 1991. A small number of cantatas by Alessandro Scarlatti have also been input in Teletau code.

Thematic Cells in German Lute Music

In an ongoing series of research projects related to the automatic transcription of German lute tablatures from the sixteenth century, Hélène Charnassé and Bernard Stepien are seeking to identify thematic cells in the development of the lute pieces. This follows their previous work, at ERATTO/C.N.R.S. in Paris, on the reconstruction of free counterpoint and *in imitatio* entries. A program written by Stepien in PROLOG detects similarities relatively easily but confronts the musicologist with some false results. For example, some cells that are indeed similar are not actually thematic cells, and the concept itself seems to want further definition.

Results can be printed on dot matrix and laser printers using Michel Wallet's *Euterpe*. A proof copy of Hans Newsidler's "Disant adiu madame" is shown in the following illustration and may be readily compared with an edited copy, in which unisons and non-calculable rests have been added, on p. 105.

The Notation of Baroque Music

A graphic lexicon of Baroque musical notation is being developed by electronically scanning selected portions of early manuscripts and editions and storing the scanned images, with documentation and commentary, in a fully indexed data base. Sorted output of images and other data is obtainable, under arbitrarily chosen headings. The project, directed by Graham Pont at the University of New South Wales, has been funded through 1990 by the Australian Research Council. Custom software by Nigel Nettheim is used.

Transcription and intabulated representation of Newsidler's "Disant adiu madame."

The *International Inventory of Villancico Texts*

An *International Inventory of Villancico Texts* was initiated recently at the State University of New York (SUNY) at Binghamton. More than 3000 examples of *pliegos sueltos*, or text booklets, each with multiple entries, survive in libraries and archives, and thousands of villancicos are preserved in manuscript in Hispanic archives. The Inventory will provide linked files for the text booklets, the manuscript sources, and the text incipits. For information on access contact Paul D. Laird, Dept. of Music, SUNY-Binghamton, Binghamton, NY 13902-6000.

A Grammar of Legrenzi's Arias

Since 1986 Mario Baroni and his collaborators have been investigating the arias of the seventeenth-century composer Giovanni Legrenzi with a view towards establishing a grammar for the works. This research, which is reported in "Relationships between Music and Poetry in the Arias of Giovanni Legrenzi (*Music and the Cognitive Sciences: Proceedings from the Symposium, 14-18 March 1988, Centre Pompidou, Paris*, ed. Stephen McAdams and Irène Delège as Vol. 4 [1989] of *Contemporary Music Review*), forms part of a larger project on the theory of European melody. The Legrenzi research has been carried out by Baroni, Rosanna Dalmonte, and Carlo Jacoboni.

Handel's Inconsistencies

Variations of note length are often found between otherwise corresponding instrumental introductions and vocal entries in the arias of Handel's operas and oratorios. In a computer analysis of incipits from 1043 arias, Graham Pont [see above] has shown that it is far more common for dots to be dropped from the vocal entries than added. This is more common in slow arias than in faster ones [Graph 1], except in 12/8, where the phenomenon is more uniform at different tempos. Pont maintains that the differences of instrumental and vocal note values in Handel's arias form part of a larger pattern of systematic variation. Vocal entries with notes of variant duration occur in 70% of the arias surveyed [Graph 2].

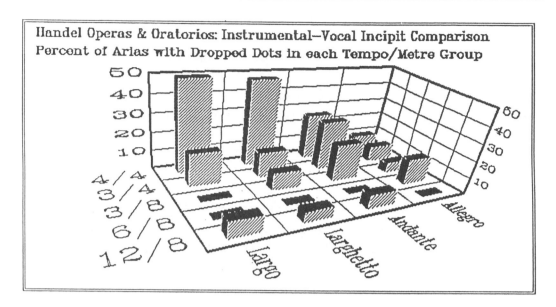

Graph 1. Profile of note-length discrepancies by meter and tempo in Handel's operas and oratorios.

Graph 2. Profile of note-length discrepancies by work. This is a chronological survey. Abbreviations for opera and oratorio titles given at the bottom should be read in zigzag fashion.

Classical and Romantic Music

Non-Musical Markings in Mozart's Autographs

Jane Perry-Camp has been constructing at Florida State University a data base and index of information concerning non-musical markings in Mozart's autographs. The meaning of these markings is thus far unexplained. In on-sight research, Perry-Camp has examined 330 autographs in the US and Europe with a view toward identifying consistent patterns, or layers of patterning, in the occurrence of these markings. A better understanding of these markings could provide insights into the habits of early copyists and the reliability of early copies, in which the markings were sometimes replicated. The flavor of the work is suggested by the profile of the string quartet K.417B shown in the following illustration.

MVMNT	MARK TYPES FOUND #	TOTAL MARKS	KIND OF MEDIUM	INK MATCH CNTXT	INK NOT MATCH CNTXT	INK AMB	% INK MAT
1	- - - 3 4 5 6 7 - 9 10 11 12	27	0 1	9	15	1	
2	- - - 3 4 - 6 - - 9 - - 12	13	0 1	5	4	1	
3	- - - - - - 6 - - 9 10 - -	4	1	3	1	0	
4	- - - - - - - - - 9 - - -	2	1	1	1	0	
5	- - - 3 4 5 6 7 - 9 10 11 12	21	0 1 2	9	8	0	
---		-----		-----	-----	----	
5 (TOTAL MVMTS IN WORK)		67		27	29	2	47

```
SUMMARY OF MARK TYPES FOR KV 417B - 1

                          ACUTE-ACCENT-SHAPED      6   =   9 % OF TOTAL MARKS
                          GRAVE-ACCENT-SHAPED      6   =   9 % OF TOTAL MARKS
                          HYPHEN-SHAPED            3   =   4 % OF TOTAL MARKS
                          DOT-SHAPED              11   =  16 % OF TOTAL MARKS
                          APOST.&VERT.-SHAPED      4   =   6 % OF TOTAL MARKS
                          MISCELLANEOUS           23   =  34 % OF TOTAL MARKS
                          PROB MOZART-MADE         7   =  10 % OF TOTAL MARKS
                          PROB INK SPLATTERS       3   =   4 % OF TOTAL MARKS
                          PROB IN PAPER ITSELF     4   =   6 % OF TOTAL MARKS
                                                 -----
                                                  67
```

```
---------------------------------------------------------------------
MATERIALS SURVEYED FOR KV 417B - 1          NUMBER OF ENTRIES
-------------------------------             -----------------
AUTOGRAPH                                          134
FIRST EDITION, NO. 1   (PARTS)                     585
HAND COPY, NO. 1       (PARTS)                      30
FIRST EDITION, NO. 2   (SCORE)                     194
---------------------------------------------------------------------
```

Non-musical markings in the autograph and early copies of Mozart's String Quartet in D Minor, K.417B.

Thematic Attributes of Schubert's Music

At the University of New South Wales in Australia Nigel Nettheim is studying compositional gestures in the themes of Schubert's music. He is building a data base of single thematic phrases encoded using *SCORE* and custom software for its interrogation and analysis.

Edvard Grieg: A Digitized Data Base of Documents

The Grieg collection in the Public Library in Bergen, Norway, includes 25,000 hand-written manuscripts by the composer and a voluminous correspondence. A data base of these documents is currently in preparation as part of the MusikkFUNN project [see p. 137]. For musical materials, the current aim is to capture as much information as possible in grey-scaled bit-mapped images. Every effort is being made to preserve differences of contrast resulting from the use of pencil and ink. For this purpose, most documents can be scanned successfully at 300 dpi. The resulting quantity of data is enormous, however, and numerous methods of data compression are being considered. For text documents such as correspondence, a modern transcription is also provided [see the following page].

It is hoped that corresponding data in different media can be made available simultaneously. Thus an interested observer might be able to see the sketch of a piano work and hear Grieg himself perform it in an original recording or to read Henrik Ibsen's letter concerning *Peer Gynt* [illustration following] while seeing a transcription of the work. The documents will be classified and catalogued according to the NORMARC-format. Distribution by electronic mail, CD-ROM, and optical disk is intended. Further information is available from Dagfinn Bach, Western Norway Research Centre, PO Box 142, N-5801 Sogndal, Norway.

Dresden den 3die Marts 1875

Kære herr Grieg !

Som svar på Deres venlige brev kan jeg idag göre Dem en meddelelse, der, efter hvad De oplyser om Kristiania theaters orkester, neppe vil være Dem uvelkommen.

Jeg kan nemlig sige Dem at "Peer Gynt" ikke påregnes til opförelse i denne spilleterminen. De vil altså have hele foråret og den störste del av sommeren til Deres rådighed. Jeg beder Dem indstændigt, ikke at göre indrømmelser lige overfor dårlige orkestertilstande. Instrumentér Deres musik efter en ideal målestokk og lad så dem deroppe sörge for at få den udført. Alt andet vilde være en mand, som Dem, uværdigt og dessuden til skade for oss begge.

I midten af April måned forlægger jeg min bolig til München, inden den tid kommer jeg rimeligvis på et par dage til Leipzig i literære forretninger. Kært skulde det være os om vi her i Dresden kunde have den fornöjelse at se Dem og Deres ærede frue forinden vor afrejse. - Med mange hilsener.

Deres venskabeligst forbundne
Henrik Ibsen

Letter from Henrik Ibsen to Edvard Grieg concerning *Peer Gynt* in Ibsen's hand (left) and in an electronic transcription (right).

American Music

Godey's *Lady's Book*

Julia Koza (author of a Ph.D. thesis on "Music and References to Music in Godey's *Lady's Book*, 1830-77," University of Minnesota, 1988) managed much of her thesis information on a data base management system called *Notebook II* (originally from Pro/Tem Software; now published by Oberon Resources), which places no limits on field size and enables every field to have text field properties. In addition to making the hardcopy version of her thesis available through University Microfilms International, she is able and willing to do searches and sorts of her data on request.

Music for Children's Choirs

Kathryn Smith's data base in Microsoft *Word* of choral works commissioned for children's choirs is available on disk or in print from the author at Webster University, St. Louis, MO 63119.

African and Afro-Latin American Rhythms

Emilio Mendoza is attempting to create a machine-readable data base of selected African and Afro-Latin American rhythmic ensemble music excerpts at the Latin American Center for Graduate Studies in Music at the Catholic University of America in Washington, D.C. Through analysis of the material collected, he hopes to develop a rhythmic and temporal grammar. He is using custom software with *Finale* on a Macintosh.

Gershwin's Piano Rolls

From 1916 to 1926 George Gershwin supported himself as an arranger of music recorded on piano rolls. When his own compositions began to reach a large audience, he curtailed his involvement with piano rolls. The rolls provide important documentation of his early development as a composer and contain much music not hitherto available in transcription.

For two years Artis Wodehouse of Palo Alto, CA, has been heading a project to generate printed scores from these rolls. In the roll technology of the 1920's, air was pumped by bellows through holes in the paper to depress notes of the player piano. Currently a video roll reader designed by David Quinlan for Micro-W in Butler, NJ, converts light emitted through these holes to machine-readable information from which synthesizer output can be generated. The synthesizer output is, in turn, converted to printed notation via *Finale*'s Enigma file format, with some fine tuning for this project.

Micro-W plans to market the Gershwin rolls for synthesizers and the Yamaha Disklavier. Wodehouse is creating editions of the previously unedited music. These will appear under the imprint of Warner Publications, Inc. Recordings of the works from new performances on a pneumatic Pianola player will appear on the Nonesuch recording label. Micro-W is located at 1342B Route 23, Butler, NJ 07405.

Address List

Aarset, Timothy, MIT Lincoln Laboratory, 244 Wood St., Lexington, MA 02173
Allsop, Peter C., Music Dept., Exeter University, Knightly, Streatham Dr., Exeter, Devon, UK,
Alphonce, Bo, Faculty of Music, McGill Univ., 555 Sherbrooke St. West, Montreal, Quebec H3A 1E3,
    Canada
Balaban, Mira, Dept. of Math. and Computer Science, Ben-Gurion University, PO Box 653,
    Beer Sheva 84105, Israel
Bamberger, Jeanne, Dept. of Music, Massachusetts Institute of Technology, Cambridge, MA 02139,
Baroni, Mario, Dip. di Musica e Spettacolo, Via Galliera, 3, I-40121 Bologna, Italy,
Bel, Bernard, Centre National de la Recherche Scientifique, 31, chemin Joseph Aiguier,
    13402 Marseille Cedex 09, France
Bent, Ian, Department of Music, Columbia University, New York, NY 10027
Binford-Walsh, Hilde, PO Box 5816, Stanford, CA 94309
Blombach, Ann K., Ohio State University, School of Music - Weigel Hall, 1866 College Road,
    Columbus, OH 43210
Böker-Heil, Norbert, Leiter, Abteilung Musikanalyse, Staat. Inst. für Musikforschung,
    Tiergarten Str. 1, D-1000 Berlin 30, Germany
Bowles, Garrett, Central Univ. Library C-075-Q, University of Calif., San Diego,
    La Jolla, CA 92093
Brinkman, Alexander, Eastman School of Music, 26 Gibbs Street, Rochester, NY 14604,
Brook, Barry, 50 Central Park West, New York, NY 10023
Butler, Malcolm, Dept. of Music, University of Hong Kong, Pokfulam Road, Hong Kong,
Byrd, Donald, P. O. Box 1571, Princeton, NJ 08542
Camilleri, Lelio, C.P. 18123, I-50129 Firenze 18, Italy
Camurri, Antonio, D.I.S.T., Università di Genova, Via Opera Pia 11A, I-16145 Genoa, Italy,
Carter, Nicholas, Music/Physics Departments, University of Surrey, Guildford, Surrey GU2 5XH, UK,
Charnassé, Hélène, CNRS-ERATTO, 27, rue Paul Bert, F-94200 Ivry-sur-Seine, France,
Cook, Nicholas, Department of Music, The University, Southampton SO9 5NH, England, UK,
Cope, David, Department of Music, University of California, Santa Cruz, CA 95064,
Dannenberg, Roger, Dept. of Computer Science, Carnegie-Mellon University, Pittsburgh, PA 15213,
Darbellay, Etienne, 40, Chemin des Limites, CH-1294 Genthod (Geneva), Switzerland,
Davis, Deta, Special Materials Cat. Div., Library of Congress, Washington, DC 20540,
De Poli, Giovanni, Istituto di Elettrotecnica, Università di Padova, Via Gradenigo, #6A,
    I-35131 Padova, Italy
Eaglestone, Barry, MMRU, Dept. of Computing, University of Bradford,
    Bradford, West Yorkshire, BD7 1DP, UK,
Ebcioglu, Kemal, IBM, T.J. Watson Research Center, P.O. Box 704, Yorktown Heights, NY 10598,
Ficici, Sevan G., 1945 Warbler, Troy, MI 48084
Finarelli, Luigi, via Corticella 68, I-40128 Bologna, Italy
Gargiulo, Piero, Via Minghetti 15, Firenze, Italy
Giannelos, Dimitris, ERATTO, 27, rue Paul-Bert, F-94200 Ivry-sur-Seine, France
Giomi, Francesco, Via Pisana 289, I-50143 Firenze, Italy
Goldfarb, Charles, IBM Almaden Research Center, 650 Harry Road, San Jose, CA 95120,
Graebner, E. M., Department of Music, University of Southampton, Highfield,
    Southampton SO9 5NH, England, UK,
Griffiths, John, Faculty of Music, University of Melbourne, Parkville, Victoria 3052, Australia,
Gross, Dorothy, ETA Systems, 5121 Colonial Drive, Golden Valley, MN 55416
Halperin, David, Dept. of Musicology, Tel Aviv University, Ramat Aviv 69 978, Tel Aviv, Israel,
Hamel, Keith A., Dept. of Music, University of British Columbia, 6361 Memorial Road,
    Vancouver, BC V6T 1W5, Canada
Haus, Goffredo, Università di Milano, Lab. di Informatica Musicale, Via Moretto da Brescia, 9,
    I-20133 Milan, Italy
Hofstetter, Fred, Dept. of Music, University of Delware, Newark, DE 19716
Holland, Simon, Institute of Educational, Technology, The Open University, Milton Keynes MK7 6AA, UK,
Hughes, Andrew, Faculty of Music, Edw. Johnson Bldg., University of Toronto, Toronto, Ont. M5S 1A1, Canada,
Inokuchi, Seiji, Dept. of Control Engineering, Faculty of Engineering Science, Osaka University,
    Toyonaka, Osaka 560, Japan
Isaacson, Eric J., 2631 E. 2nd St., #10, Bloomington, IN 47401
Janzen, J., 1122 Casson Green N.W., Calgary, AB T3B 2V6, Canada
Jesser, Barbara, Universitat Essen - Hochschule, PB 4, Musik, D-4300 Essen 1, Germany,
Katayose, Haruhiro, Dept. of Control Engineering, Faculty of Engineering Science,
    Osaka University, Toyonaka, Osaka 560, Japan
Keller, Kate and Robert, 13125 Scarlet Oak Dr., Darnestown, MD 20878

Kippen, James, Dept. of Soc. Anthropology, Queen's University, Toronto M5S 1A5, Canada,
Klir, George, Dept. of Systems Science, State University of New York, Binghamton, NY 13901,
Koza, Julia, 5554 Humanities Bldg., Univ. of Wisconsin, 455 N. Park St., Madison, WI 53706,
Lancashire, Ian, c/o University of Toronto, 14th Floor, Robarts Library, 130 St. George St.,
  Toronto, Ont. M5S 1A5, Canada
LaRue, Jan, Woods End Rd., New Canaan, CT 06840-4030
Laske, Otto, 926 Greendale Ave., Needham, MA 02192
Leman, Marc, University of Ghent, Seminar of Musicology, IPEM, Blandijnberg 2, B-9000 Ghent, Belgium,
Lincoln, Harry B., Dept. of Music, State University of New York, Binghamton, NY 13901,
Lischka, Christoph, Gesellsch. für Mathematik, und Datenverarbeitung, Postfach 1240,
  D-5205 St. Augustin 1, Germany
Lister, Craig, Manhattan School of Music, 120 Claremont Avenue, New York, NY 10027,
Marsden, Alan A., Department of Music, The Queen's University, Belfast BT7 1NN, Northern Ireland, UK,
Massi, R. Wood, 4314 Nineteenth Street, San Francisco, CA 94114
McGee, William F., Dept. of Electrical Engineering, University of Ottawa, 770 King Edward Avenue,
  Ottawa, Ont. K1N 6N5, Canada
Mendoza, Emilio, 8605 Flower Ave. #2, Takoma Park, MD 20912-6633
Merkley, Paul, Dept. of Electrical Engineering, University of Ottawa, 770 King Edward Avenue,
  Ottawa, Ont. K1N 6N5, Canada
Morehen, John, Department of Music, University Park, Nottingham NG7 2RD, England, UK,
Nettheim, Nigel, 204A Beecroft Road, Cheltenham NSW 2119, Australia
Newcomb, Steven R., Center for Music Research, Florida State University, Tallahassee, FL 32306,
Nordli, Kjell E., Department of Informatics, University of Oslo, P.O. Box 1080, Blindern,
  N-0316 Oslo 3, Norway
Ohteru, Sadamu, Dept. of Applied Physics, Waseda University, 3-4-1 Okubo, Shinjuku-ku,
  Tokyo 160, Japan
Perry-Camp, Jane, School of Music, The Florida State University, Tallahassee, FL 32306-2098,
Peters, G. David, CERL Music Group, Univ. of Illinois, 103 S. Mathews #252, Urbana, IL 61801-2977,
Plenkers, Leo J., Inst. voor Muziekwetenschap, Universiteit van Amsterdam, Spuistraat 134 Kr. 718,
  1012 VB Amsterdam, NL
Pont, Graham, Dept. of General Studies, University of New South Wales, P.O. Box 1,
  Kensington NSW 2033, Australia
Pople, Anthony, Department of Music, University of Lancaster, Lancaster, LA1 4YW, UK,
Rabson, Carolyn, 67 King St., Oberlin, OH 44074
Rahn, John, Department of Music, University of Washington, Seattle, WA 98195
Reis, Joan S., 2200 Victory Pkwy., #2507, Cincinnati, OH 45206
Rhodes, James C., Shorter College, Box 387, Rome, GA 30161-4298
Schaffer, John William, School of Music, Univ. of Wisconsin, 455 N. Park Street,
  Madison, WI 53706
Schaffrath, Helmut, Universität Essen, FB 4, Musik, D-4300 Essen 1, Germany
Sitter, Peer, Sauerbruchstr. 34, D-4900 Herford, Germany
Stinson, John, Music Department, La Trobe University, Bundoora, Victoria 3083, Australia,
Trowbridge, Lynn, 4029 Autumn Ct., Fairfax, VA 22030
Vollsnes, Arvid, Department of Music, University of Oslo, P.O. Box 1017 Blindern,
  N-0315 Oslo 3, Norway
Wallet, Michel, 88, rue Frideric Nistral, F-03700 Montluçon, France
Waters, William J., Reference Librarian, Pensacola Junior College, 1000 College Blvd.,
  Pensacola, FL 32504
Wenker, Jerome, 3522 Skycroft Drive, St. Anthony Village, MN 55418
Whistlecroft, Lisa, CTICM, Lancaster University, Lancaster LA1 4YW, UK
Winter, Robert, Dept. of Music, University of California, 405 Hilgard Ave., Los Angeles, CA 90024,
Wittlich, Gary, School of Music, Indiana University, Bloomington, IN 47405
Wodehouse, Artis, 3974 Park Blvd., Palo Alto, CA 94306
Wu, Stephen, Dept. of Computer Science, University of Hong Kong, Hong Kong
Zannos, Ioannis, RCAST, Oshuga Laboratory, University of Tokyo, 4-6-1 Komaba, Meguro-ku,
  Tokyo 153, Japan

Index

Mendoza, Emilio 153
Mensural notation 26, 72, 73, 133
  encoding of 27
  red 34
  systems for printing 34
  white 26, 27, 33, 65
Mergenthaler 63
Merkley, Paul 42
Mesopotamia 145
Messenger, T. 37
Micro-W 154
Middleton, David 46
MIDI 14-8, 51, 57, 63-65, 67-69, 71-73, 112, 115-
  6, 121, 123-4, 127-8, 139-41
  file format 51
Miller, Jim 69
Miller, Karl 141
Minds and Machines 15
MIPS
  secretariat 56
Modelling 10
  of compositional process 120
  of music theory 118
  of musical cognition 15
  of non-harmonic tones 16
  musical knowledge acquisition 126
Models of Musical Communication and Cognition 15
Monday, Jon 140
Monophonic repertories 24
Montel, Dominique 63, 86, 96
Moore School of Electrical Engineering 107
Morehen, John 24, 65
Morris, R. J. 18
Morris, Robert 17
Mould, Charles 135
Mozart, W. A.
  autographs 150
  keyboard sonatas 122
  Magic Flute 141
MS DOS 71, 120, 126
MTeX 67
MUSED 67
Music Analysis System 116
Music Catalogue of the Netherlands 134
Music Cataloguing Collection (OCLC) 134
Music Data 140
Music theory 123, 125
  treatises 132-3
Music4C 124
Musical Cultures of the World 142
Musical information
  processing standards for 53-6
  theories of 122
MusicLogo 121
MusicPrinter 116
Music Manuscriptor 67, 80, 87
Music Publisher 67
Music software catalogues 13

Music Teaching and Learning 9
Music Theory Spectrum 12
Music V 17
Musical abstraction 12
Musical data 12, 139-40
The Musical Quarterly 46
Musical structure 17, 110
Musicology 12, 14, 16, 18, 128
MusicPrinter Plus 61, 68
MusicProse 66
Musicus 12, 62
Musicwriter II 68
MusikkFUNN 151
MusiKrafters 68
Musikus 62, 137
MusScribe 68
MUSTRAN 68
Nahay, Paul 71
National Center for Machine-Readable Texts 19
National Centre of Music Technology 137
National Endowment for the Humanities 56
National Information Services Corp. 135
National Tune Index 138
Near-Eastern traditional music 120
Nettheim, Nigel 146, 151
Neue Mozart Ausgabe 73
Neumes 23-7, 26, 35, 42, 70
Neural nets 9, 14, 17, 18
New York University 134
Newcomb, Steven R. 53
NeWS 62
Newsidler, Hans 105, 146, 147
NeXT 12, 66, 131
Nightingale 68
Nordli, Kjell E. 51
NORMARC-format 151
North Texas State University 117
Notation 62
  Baroque 146
  interface 10
  research 14, 62
  semiotic study of 17
  software 61-106
  syntax 62
The Note Processor 42, 61, 62, 64, 69, 90, 101,
  128
Notebook II 153
Note-list 128
Notes 61
NoteWriter 62, 69
Nottingham University 24
Nuance 42
Oberon Music Editor 62, 69, 76, 83
Object-oriented data definition 122
Objectworks 18
OCLC 134
Octave transposition 52
Odington, Walter 132

A Note to Contributors

Computing in Musicology welcomes information on current and recent academic research and software development. We accept material from diverse disciplines. Contributors of technical and scientific material should seek to emphasize the value of their work in musical studies. Contributors of historical, theoretical, and analytical applications are encouraged to state how their work is related to other computer-assisted work with similar goals and how their approach could be adapted to other topics. Illustrations that capture the essence of the capability described are highly desirable.

Contributions of more than a few pages should be accompanied by an abstract. Contributions of any length in languages other than English, French, German, or Italian should be accompanied by a résumé in English. Almost all material reported in *Computing in Musicology* is significantly condensed, and it is therefore to the contributor's advantage to provide succinct information.

Those wishing to be included in the solicitation for contributions of output from notational software programs should contact the Center by March 31. All other contributions must be received by June 30. All contributions should be addressed to *Computing in Musicology*, Center for Computer Assisted Research in the Humanities, 525 Middlefield Road, Suite 120, Menlo Park, CA 94025. Short contributions without illustrations may be sent by electronic mail (xb.l36@Stanford.bitnet) or by fax (415-329-8365); these should be identified clearly as contributions to *Computing in Musicology* and must be accompanied by a complete name, mailing address, and telephone number.

We are unable to guarantee mention of every contribution. Contributions unused in the year of their submission may play a role in determining the coverage of future issues. Only contributions including specially prepared materials can be acknowledged.

We thank you for your patience and cooperation.

Order Form
Computing in Musicology

Name: _____

Address: _____

_____

_____

_____

Telephone: _____ **Fax:** _____

Prepaid orders only.　　　　　　　　　　　　　　*Federal ID # 94-3038594*

Postage and handling charges:

To addresses in the United States and Canada—$2.00 per order up to three copies; $1.00 each additional copy.

To all other addresses by surface mail—$3.00 per order up to three copies; $1.00 each additional copy.

To Europe by air—$8.00 postage and handling per item. To Asia, Africa, South America, Australia, New Zealand, and the U.S.S.R. by air—$10.00 postage and handling per item.

Methods of payment:

All payments must be in $US paid by check through an American bank or by postal money order.
All checks should be made out to **CCARH**.

ISBN	Year	Price	No.	Postage	Total Amt.
0-936943-05-X	**1990**	$18.00			
0-936943-04-1	**1989**	$15.00			
0-936943-03-3	**1988**	$12.00			
0-936943-02-5	**1987**	$10.00			
Total items, handling					
Total amount enclosed					

Please return to:

Computing in Musicology
Center for Computer Assisted Research in the Humanities
525 Middlefield Road, Suite 120
Menlo Park, CA 94025

Telephone: (415) 322-7050　　　　　　　　　　*Fax:* (415) 329-8365